DUBLIN CASTLE
and the 1916 RISING

DUBLIN CASTLE

and

THE 1916 RISING

by

LEON Ó BROIN

SIDGWICK & JACKSON

LONDON

SBN 283 98094 X

Made and Printed in Great Britain by
The Garden City Press Limited
Letchworth, Hertfordshire
for Sidgwick and Jackson Limited
1 Tavistock Chambers, Bloomsbury Way
London W.C.1

Contents

ACKNOWLEDGEMENTS

page 7

DUBLIN CASTLE AND THE 1916 RISING

page 9

REFERENCES

page 179

SOURCES

page 186

INDEX

page 189

List of Plates

(between pages 96 and 97)

1 'NATHAN THE UNWISE'
Sir Matthew Nathan – Under Secretary for Ireland

2 PAGEANTRY OF BRITISH RULE
British cavalry during the state entry of the Viceroy, Lord Wimborne, into Dublin Castle in 1914

3 DUBLIN CASTLE – CENTRE OF BRITISH RULE
The Upper Gate, showing the guardroom on the right

4 IRELAND'S RULERS
Sir Matthew Nathan and Augustine Birrell together in 1916

5 AFTERMATH
Scene of devastation around the G.P.O., which was the rebel headquarters. Only a matter of days before this photograph was taken the rebel flag flew over the building

6 AFTERMATH
Sackville Street and Eden Quay. The G.P.O. cannot be seen but it is on the left of Nelson's column (which is on left of picture)

7 DRAMATIS PERSONAE
Top row (left to right): General Sir John Maxwell; John Dillon, Irish Nationalist leader; Augustine Birrell, Chief Secretary for Ireland. Bottom row: Lord Wimborne, Viceroy; Herbert Asquith, British Prime Minister; John Redmond, Irish Nationalist leader

Acknowledgements

It will be apparent to the reader that I have depended very largely for the material on which this book is based on the Nathan and Asquith papers in the Bodleian Library, and on an account of his 1916 experiences in Dublin written by the late A. H. Norway. For permission to examine and use these papers I most gratefully acknowledge my indebtedness to the Bodleian and Mr. D. S. Porter of its Department of Western Manuscripts; to the late Mr. E. J. Nathan; to Mr. Mark Bonham Carter; and to Mrs. F. M. Norway. I am also obliged to Mrs. Eibhlin Tierney for permission to make use, to the extent I have done, of her father's (Eoin MacNeill) papers, and likewise to Dr. Liam Price for putting Sir Matthew Nathan's letters to Dorothy Stopford at my disposal. I am particularly happy to have Miss Margaret Pearse's consent to the publication of the letter and poems in the Asquith papers, written by her brother, P. H. Pearse, before his execution.

I have been facilitated in various respects in my researching by Colonel Robert J. Stopford, J. Y. Bell, Sir David Lidbury, Lord Hurcomb, Alan Wolstencroft, L. G. Hart, Mrs. Amber Blanco White, Very Rev. J. R. MacMahon, S.J., Nuala Moran, the late J. W. O'Neill, Joseph Brennan, G. C. Duggan, Major Florence O'Donoghue, and Joan Lally, as well as by the Director of Public Relations (Army) of the British Ministry of Defence, and by the Librarians and library staffs of the National Library of Ireland, Trinity College, Dublin, the Dublin Corporation, the Royal Dublin Society and the Irish Central Library for Students. To all these kind people I return sincere thanks.

Dublin
June, 1970

LEON Ó BROIN

CHAPTER ONE

Things could not have been quieter in Dublin Castle, the traditional centre of British power in Ireland, than they were on Easter Monday morning, 1916. It was a Bank Holiday of course; the Civil Servants had the day off; and the handful of police and military on duty, with little to do, had time to lament that they could not enjoy the summer weather that had come so soon, and join, as some of them would have liked, the crowds that were already making their way to the Fairyhouse races. About ten o'clock the constable at the Upper Gate saw Sir Matthew Nathan pass in and saluted him. He was not surprised to see him because everybody knew the Under-Secretary's passion for work. When everybody else went home on an ordinary evening at four or five o'clock, Sir Matthew invariably stayed on, tied to his desk, doing God knows what.

More than an hour later this Easter Monday morning, Sir Matthew was followed into the Castle by Major Ivor Price, the Military Intelligence Officer. There was serious business to be done involving the arrest of a large number of Sinn Féiners who, in active co-operation with the King's enemies, had been planning rebellion. For some time the two men discussed the position and then Nathan phoned the General Post Office and asked the Secretary, Arthur Hamilton Norway, to come to the Castle at once.

Norway saw nothing unusual as he hurried through the city streets. He surmized that he was required in connection with a matter that Sir Matthew had mentioned to him a couple of days earlier. A 'prisoner of consequence' had been arrested in Kerry, and some risk existed of an attempt at rescuing him as he was brought through Dublin on his way to London. Nathan confirmed to Norway as soon as he entered the room that the prisoner was in fact Sir Roger Casement and that he had been

9

successfully conveyed to London under guard, with no attempt at rescue. Further action was now called for and he wanted immediate steps taken for denying the use of the telephone and telegraph service over large areas of the South of Ireland for all but military and naval use. Needing a written order, Norway was actually composing it for Nathan's signature when a volley of musketry crashed out beneath the window. Norway, startled, looked up. 'What's that?' he asked. 'Oh that's probably the attack the Sinn Féiners have been promising on the Castle' cried Nathan, jumping up and running from the room. Major Price shouted from the window to some person below, after which he too ran off. Norway made his way downstairs. At the foot of the staircase he found all the messengers huddled together, frightened out of their wits. They had just seen the policeman at the gate shot through the heart.

They had managed however to shut the gate of the Upper Castle Yard, and the gate of the lower yard was closed almost simultaneously. The military guard at the Upper Gate had been overwhelmed but the attackers had then withdrawn. Nathan, with the storekeeper, broke open the armoury in the hope of arming whatever constables were within the Castle area, but while he found some revolvers, there were no cartridges for them, and later he remembered that few of the Dublin police knew anything about firearms. Price, meanwhile, had alerted Military Headquarters by telephone. The rebellion had started. Downtown one important building after another was seized, barricades were thrown up, the Union Jack was hauled down from the G.P.O. and the green flag of the Irish Republic now floated in its place over the rebel headquarters.

CHAPTER TWO

The ancestors of the Under-Secretary, Sir Matthew Nathan, are believed to have come from Dessau in Germany. One of them was a cutter of quill pens and through him there developed the firm of Nathan and Sons which had premises in Whitechapel in the East of London. When this firm later ceased to exist one of the family joined Thomas de la Rue who had the contract for the supply of quills to the Bank of England, so that when, more than a hundred years later, Nathan incorporated three pens in the device on his shield on becoming High Sheriff of Somerset, he was recalling the occupation of his forebears.

Nathan was born on 3 January 1862, of Jonah Nathan's second marriage to Miriam Jacobs. Both parents were of Jewish families, long established in England, and were 'both characterized by an entirely British outlook'. At this time Jewish boys were not welcomed at the best English public schools and Mrs Nathan had to rely on a mathematics tutor and a succession of foreign governesses as well as on visiting masters from a nearby 'crammers' establishment for the education of her eight children. They all did well and Matthew, on entering the Royal Military Academy, Woolwich, as a cadet, distinguished himself and went on to receive the sword of honour at the passing-out examination. He was commissioned in the Royal Engineers at the age of eighteen and was employed for a while in the fortifications branch of the War Office, before being sent on foreign service. At Sierra Leone he designed the fortifications which were to convert the harbour into a coasting station. He was in Egypt and the Sudan for a year at the time of the first struggle with the Mahdi and helped to construct a railway across the Nile. Later he spent three years in India and Burma on the erection of coast defences, and took part in an expedition in the Lushai hills where he won a medal and promotion. He returned to

England in 1891 and for most of the following decade he was at the War Office, either in the fortifications branch or as Secretary to the Colonial Defence Committee, in which capacity he played a part in a Conference of Premiers, over which Joseph Chamberlain presided.

At the instance of the Colonial Office, he then returned to Sierra Leone as acting Governor and within a year was given a similar post on the Gold Coast. He held this job for over six years and took away to Hong Kong with him and later to Natal the reputation of being a wise and zealous reformer. He was Governor of Natal with the rank of lieutenant-colonel until the formation of the Union of South Africa. This event brought him back to England where his spectacular series of appointments was continued. He became in succession Secretary to the Post Office and Chairman of the Board of Inland Revenue.(1) Lloyd George, who was Chancellor of the Exchequer at the time, had a high regard for Nathan's capacity and may have had something to say to it when, shortly after the declaration of war against Germany in August 1914, Nathan was designated Under-Secretary for Ireland and a member of the Irish Privy Council. There had been trouble in Dublin over an attempt to prevent a party of Irish Volunteers carrying away arms that had been surreptitiously landed, and changes in the Irish administration were considered necessary.

Nathan was fifty-two by now, and was unmarried. Not that he was not interested in women – he was and had close friends among them. Among these were Violet Asquith, the Prime Minister's brilliant daughter (1a); Amber Blanco White, the Fabian beauty who figured in the plays of Shaw and the novels of Wells; Constance Heppell-Marr (a daughter of George Fletcher, the English assistant secretary of the Irish Department of Agriculture and Technical Instruction); and Mary Kingsley (the explorer and naturalist) who conceived an affection for him which he did not return. She admired his courage, the soldier in him, and the fact that he was a Jew. Women, generally, appear to have found him attractive. In appearance he was rather like the playwright Synge; upright, square-shouldered, powerfully built with a finely shaped head and strong jaw while his blue-grey eyes and his resonant voice revealed a forceful but pleasant personality. As a young man he tried unsuccessfully on a couple of occasions to marry within the Jewish community; in later life, a permanent matrimonial arrangement was possibly unthinkable for so totally devoted a servant of the public, or maybe, as has been suggested, he grew to have respect for women only so long as they were useful to him.(2).

He had been to Ireland before more than once. In January 1911, he attended the Irish Post Office Annual Dinner in Dublin and made an excellent speech. In the following year he stayed as one of an Easter party with the Lyttletons in the Royal Hospital in Kilmainham, the official residence of the Officer Commanding in Chief in Ireland. Lady Gregory was there, and W. B. Yeats, telling how once he found George Russell (A.E.) at Lady Gregory's place in Galway embracing a tree because his spirit had been called up into the sap. The new Treasury Remembrancer, Maurice Headlam, was also among the guests, and found the Home Rule atmosphere uncongenial. Nathan told him on that occasion that he had had seven appointments in ten years but had sought none of them; he had adopted the old rule of never asking for anything and always accepting what was offered. Headlam did not know why Nathan was such a friend of Lady Lyttleton's but he was 'notoriously able and thoroughly nice, without being effusive'. He came down to breakfast one morning in the middle of prayers, plumped down on his knees, and joined in the responses, from which Headlam assumed that he had left Judaism. He did not put in an appearance, however, at the service on Good Friday.(3) But wherever his religious allegiance at that time lay, Nathan was active in Jewish circles later on in life and was buried as a Jew.

He was an uncommonly good man, accessible, hospitable and the possessor of a marked gift for friendship. The Under-Secretaryship to which he had been appointed carried £2,000 a year as well as the residence in the Phoenix Park beside the Viceregal Lodge now occupied by the Papal Nuncio, and Nathan seems to have been in the habit of giving away somewhat more than a fifth of his salary. He may have had some money of his own, of course, but he was naturally kind and generous, as well as being pleasant as a chief and willing as a subordinate. He had unlimited initiative and drive and an unequalled capacity for working hard over long stretches. In fact, he was a model public official and it looked when he became the permanent head of the Irish government service at this period of political transition as if nothing could prevent him from being an outstanding success. It was admittedly a difficult job to supervise 'the great Irish experiment' of Home Rule but if he could not do it, who could?

The *Irish Times* thought that an Irishman should have been given this task but they had to acknowledge their confidence in Nathan because of his meteoric achievements in other fields (5 October 1914). The *Freeman's Journal* which, as the organ of the Irish Parliamentary Party, should have known, declared that Nathan was the personal selection of the Prime Minister; he had been chosen because of his special fitness for the duties that would devolve on him, and 'when his record was examined his selection would be understood'. The national periodicals were critical. D. P. Moran of *The Leader* announced that the appointment of 'Sir Matt' as 'the head bottle-washer in the Irish government'(4) and his assignment had been received 'with amazement and stupefaction'. He was probably a Mason as well as a Jew and the only experience he could claim as a qualification to rule the Irish was that he had earlier been a governor of yellow and black-skinned races.(5) Moran also alleged that Nathan was a first cousin of an ex-mayor of Rome who had earned notoriety because of the bitterness of his attacks on the Catholic Church. This was denied in the *Freeman,* however, as one of the many fabrications that were being used to discredit the government that had given Home Rule to Ireland; and Moran withdrew the accusation. Nathan appears to have ignored these particular criticisms but he was hurt when Tim Healy called him a *German* Jew. He made no public refutation of this, for it might have been difficult to do so, but he subsequently refused to do any business with Healy.

A couple of years before this, another higher Civil Servant had run into much more serious trouble on arriving in Dublin. This was Arthur Hamilton Norway who was put in charge of the Irish Post Office. He was greeted with a storm of protest which, beginning in *The Leader* and *Sinn Féin,* spread to the local authorities, some of which passed resolutions expressing their disgust at the promotion of an English Protestant and Mason to the exclusion of able Catholic officials like James McMahon. There was a conspiracy afoot, the *Leader* alleged, involving Samuel, 'the Jew financier' who was Postmaster-General, and Birrell, 'the intellectual coon' who was Chief Secretary for Ireland; a conspiracy that made a mockery of Home Rule.

All of this was very wide of the mark, however. In 1912 Norway had been one of the Assistant Secretaries at the Headquarters of the Post Office in London; the Dublin appointment was of rather lower standing although it carried the same salary, and could not be offered to him as a promotion. Indeed a son of his, who distinguished himself later as the novelist Nevil Shute, thought the Dublin job was somewhat of a dead end and that his father had taken it because of an increasing deafness.(6)

Norway had served under Nathan at Post Office Headquarters and their relations had not been free from friction: but they had met with cordiality at a dinner in London just before the outbreak of the war and it was on that occasion that Norway learned that Nathan was coming to Dublin as Under-Secretary, and would be his superior once more. He invited him to come and stay with him at South Hill, Blackrock, until the Under-Secretary's Lodge was ready and advised him to have nothing to do with the Kildare Street Club. 'In the minds of Nationalists it is identified irreparably with a narrow and rather bitter type of Unionism which they resent. Rightly or wrongly, the feeling exists, to an extent which is worth attention from an Englishman taking up duty here for the first time and hoping, as I presume you do, to occupy a position of friendly relations with both sides.'(7) Norway saw Nathan as 'a man of charming manners, to dine with whom was a very agreeable experience, since he was a courteous and polished host and had the instinct for entertaining'. But he lacked discernment and resolution, he thought. 'What is the use', Nathan once said, 'of contending against the stream of tendency?' 'That is fatalism', Norway suggested. 'No,' Nathan replied, 'it is good sense.' And Nathan's conception of loyalty, according to Norway, was not to correct his political chief when he found him going wrong, but to help him in his policy without remonstrance whatever form it took. In thus behaving, Norway saw Nathan acting as a soldier rather than as a civil servant occupying an important post.

Nathan had therefore his critics in the Irish Civil Service from the day he arrived. It did not help when he brought a private secretary named Kurten with him from Somerset House, an Englishman who was young enough to be in the forces. But this apart, there was a tendency to look askance at Nathan. A few of the senior officers liked him, because he had a kindly way with them, but others thought they saw him regarding them and their department with a fine Semitic scorn, with a kind of patient tolerance which they found amusing in one who knew so little about the country. They found it hard also to understand what it was kept him busy from half past nine in the morning until seven in the evening when his predecessors had been able to get through the work in a few hours. And his habit, after an interview, of writing a full statement of his recollection of what had passed, and of producing it afterwards to refute some point under discussion embarrassed them, and inspired them to write their own accounts of what had transpired so as to be ready for any eventuality.(8) This was what Sir Henry Robinson, perhaps the ablest official of them all, thought and did.

Others, particularly Headlam the Treasury Remembrancer, criticised Nathan because he was such a strong politician, which meant, of course, that his brand of politics was different from theirs. He was a Liberal, and they, Tories. He had committed the cardinal sin of not joining the Kildare Street Club of which all the best people, including the higher Civil Servants, were members, and of going openly to visit John Dillon, the Nationalist M.P., about Irish affairs. He was such a nice chap, however, that they were disposed to blame his political superior Augustine Birrell, the Chief Secretary, for these aberrations. Birrell, they all agreed, was indolent and inert; and they judged this by the fact that he only came to Dublin occasionally, had given up using the Chief Secretary's Lodge since his wife's death and kept to himself a lot, taking his meals in indifferent restaurants instead of going to a club. But Birrell conceived it to be of the nature of the Chief Secretary's job that he should spend most of his time in London. Attending the Cabinet and Parliament demanded this of him, if only to ensure that Irish interests were not overlooked; and his most recent distinguished Tory predecessor, A. J. Balfour, had only spent six months in all in Ireland in four and a half years. There was a private wire to the Irish Office in London and continuous communication with

Dublin Castle; and Birrell claimed that in the London office he had 'all the machinery of government' at his disposal, the papers, a library, a private draughtsman, his own private secretary, and long correspondence on most private and confidential subjects.

The policy to which Birrell introduced Nathan was to pave the way for Home Rule and make any other solution of the Irish political problem impossible. Apart from the Home Rule measure, he had carried no fewer than fifty-five Bills through the House of Commons, dealing with such subjects as land purchase, housing and the National University. He sought, through the exercise of his patronage, to give the Irish Catholic a larger say in the affairs of his country and he was especially alive to the need to change the image that Dublin Castle, the seat of government, presented to the generality of Irishmen. 'It is not', he said in 1907, 'that Dublin Castle is a sink of jobbery and corruption, but it is, to use a familiar expression "switched off" from the current of National life and feeling. No pulse of real life beats in its breast. The main currents of Irish thought as they surge round its walls pass almost unheeded.'(9) This was essentially true but to seek to change the position did not endear Birrell to the Tory-minded official. When first appointed, Birrell knew nothing about Ireland but he read widely in Irish history from Edmund Spencer through Lecky to John Mitchel and Michael Davitt, as well as the Irish novelists and novels about Ireland, and the political speeches on Irish affairs(10) while his perusal of the monthly reports of the Royal Irish Constabulary gave him a real insight into 'the habits, customs and pastimes of almost every village in the land'.

Nathan followed Birrell's example. He read any books about Ireland he could lay his hands on – in his first days in Dublin, apart from historical works, he read some published Abbey plays among them T. C. Murray's *Maurice Harte,* St. John Ervine's *Mixed Marriage* and J. M. Synge's *The Sorrows of Deirdre.* He went about making contact with the 'right' people, the nation- ally-minded people, and in almost his first letter from Dublin he suggested to Lloyd George to come over and spend a few days 'absorbing Irish sentiment' as if he had begun to absorb it him- self. This, he thought, would prompt Lloyd George to make the sort of speech that would gain a large mass of public opinion both in Ireland and America for the duration of the war and after it.(*11*) Nathan was keen on getting at what the Irish were thinking and looking for but he did not look far or deeply enough, for neither he nor his mentor realized the kind of men that had now appeared on the scene. A new generation had arisen of young men and women, Gaelic Leaguers rather than Land Leaguers, to whom the old Parliamentary machine seemed old-fashioned, slow-going and out of date, and its leaders out of sympathy with, and – dangerous error – inclined to snub the young. This generation was intensely disloyal to the English connection. 'But then,' said Birrell, 'nobody in Ireland, North or South, save a handful of officials was, or ever had been, loyal to England in the true sense of the word.'(*12*).

CHAPTER THREE

It was evident from an early stage that the war with Germany would be a long and bloody business, and Ireland was expected to contribute her quota to the new armies that were being got ready. Recruiting was, therefore, a matter of major concern to Nathan but recruiting could not be successfully carried out without reducing the tremendous tensions over the issue of Home Rule and creating some sense of unity between North and South, between Unionists and Nationalists. Home Rule was on the Statute Book as a result of the combined effort of the Liberals and the Irish Parliamentary Party but had been suspended for the duration of the war in circumstances that made it likely that if ever it became operative, it would be on the basis of the separation of most of the Northern Counties from the rest of the country. In support of the agitation against Home Rule nearly half a million Ulstermen and women had signed a covenant to oppose the measure by force, an Ulster Volunteer Force had been formed and armed with guns, illegally imported, while a suggestion that they would be expected to disarm the Ulstermen had stirred up something akin to a revolt among the British Army Officers at the Curragh. This was an Ulster rebellion; of that the law officers had no doubt, but where or how the rebels were to be tried and how many of them should be put in the dock were the most difficult questions to answer. The consequences of not doing anything were obvious to everybody but, said Birrell, 'politics often consists of balancing one set of grave evils against another set, and after consideration the cabinet, with my concurrence, decided to leave it alone, although by doing nothing they almost negatived their right to be called a "Government" at all'.(*1*)

The lesson of all this had not been lost on the Nationalists of the South; they had promptly proceeded to form their own

Volunteer force and had likewise resorted to gun-running to arm themselves; but in the process of bringing the guns into Dublin on a Sunday afternoon the military at Bachelor's Walk shot down some civilians who indulged in cat-calls from the pavements. The contrast was there for everybody to see. The British Army Officer class and the higher Civil Service, Unionists for the most part, could be relied on to discriminate against Nationalist and Liberal opinion. Nathan's role was to correct this attitude as best he could so as to give the people of Ireland the feeling that they were being fairly governed and the way prepared for the transfer of government to them.

A factor of some importance in the situation was the rise of Labour, under the demagogic leadership of James Larkin. His power over the working classes was quite fantastic and he must have perturbed the Authorities exceedingly when, following the great 1913 lockout, he began to speak as a Nationalist rather than as a Socialist and to organize gigantic anti-war demonstrations at which he denounced those who encouraged Irishmen to enlist in the British Army. The Irish Nationalist Leader, John Redmond, was an 'Irish Judas' and he wondered if there was no one to provide a rope and a tree to hang him, for he had betrayed the Nation as Christ was betrayed.(2) When, a little later, Larkin went to America, the Government were suspicious about his motives in going there and wanted to know how he was being financed. In time, they had more reason, however, to be concerned with one of Larkin's colleagues, James Connolly, a man of quite extraordinary determination who, in addition to being a Trade Union leader and the editor of a Trade Union journal, commanded a small Citizen Army that was brought into being to protect the workers against the police, for, as had happened in connection with the arming of the Volunteer forces, the police had been employed with brutality against the wretchedly paid workers in 1913.

A further matter of concern to the British to which Nathan's attention was directed at an early stage was the behaviour of Roger Casement, a pensioned member of their Foreign Office staff. They had knighted him for his services in the Congo and Putamayo where he had exposed the exploitation of the native rubber workers, and allowed him to retire on health grounds. Casement did not want the decoration but found it difficult to refuse it. He had become a separatist and a friend of Bulmer Hobson of the secret Irish Republican Brotherhood. Out of his limited means he had generously supported the Irish-Ireland movements of the day including the novel school with its roots in the Gaelic past that P. H. Pearse had started in a Dublin suburb; and, when the Irish Volunteer movement began, he supported it enthusiastically and helped to plan the Howth gun-running. He foresaw the 1914–18 war and was strongly convinced that Ireland's best chance of becoming an independent republic lay in the victory of the Central Powers. He was in the United States campaigning among the Irish Americans on behalf of the Volunteers when hostilities actually broke out, and went to Germany where he secured a declaration that the German government desired Ireland to be free and that German troops, if they ever reached the shores of Ireland, would come inspired by goodwill. Later he entered into an agreement which cleared the way for the organizing of an Irish Brigade in Germany from among the Irishmen in the British Army who had been taken prisoners in the fighting in Flanders. Some of these moves were given publicity at home and were understandably regarded as rank treachery by the British. Their Minister in Christiania in Norway tried to dispose of Casement on his way into Germany by having him knocked over the head and dropped into the waters of a fiord.

Nathan had already some idea of the organization of government in Ireland. At the top was what was known as the Executive, consisting of a Lord Lieutenant, his Chief Secretary and his Under-Secretary, the first two being politicians and the third a Civil Servant. The Lord Lieutenant was notionally responsible for the civil government in the country while the military forces of the Crown in Ireland were under his orders. But, when as in 1914, the Chief Secretary was in the Cabinet and the Lord Lieutenant was not, responsibility was in practice vested in the Chief Secretary and was discharged very largely for him by the permanent Under-Secretary who, we may remind ourselves, was now Nathan. The policy of the Chief Secretary was the policy of the British Government as a whole, and it was obviously impossible that there should be any other independent authority or responsibility in Ireland. For many years the office of Lord

Lieutenant had therefore been a ceremonial office. It was an anomalous system which worked fairly enough in quiet times but proved to be almost unworkable in times of stress. R. Barry O'Brien put it well when he said that the Lord Lieutenant wore the insignia of command and signed the log, but the Chief Secretary was really the Captain of the ship, while the Under-Secretary was the man at the wheel.(3)

Lord Aberdeen was the Viceroy at the end of 1914 but was on his way out. He could not go fast enough for Birrell, however, who saw in him a rather ridiculous figure who was unable or unwilling to control his wife who continually interfered with public departments in matters for which she had no responsibility. She was a well-intentioned busybody but her desire for power, influence and patronage led to much unpleasantness. Birrell's feelings are reflected in the very first reference to Aberdeen in Nathan's papers: 'I see the *Outgoing Tenant* is detained by stress of weather,' Birrell told Nathan, 'but I suppose his departure cannot be long delayed. After making such a shower of Knights: and of the kind we lawyers call *remanets,* he can hardly protract his stay in a city he has done so much to make absurd.'(4) There were people however, who made Birrell share this absurdity as, for instance, the wag who saw Ireland as 'an island ruled by a harmless Earl and an innocent Essayist'.(5)

The Irish Executive or Irish Government – both terms were employed – had its headquarters at the Chief Secretary's Office in Dublin Castle. In the same building were accommodated the law officers who traditionally were considered to share the government with the Executive. Immediately under the control of the Executive were the two police forces, the Royal Irish Constabulary (R.I.C.) and the Dublin Metropolitan Police (D.M.P.), and a number of departments such as the General Registry Office and the General Prisons Board. The Chief Secretary was also *ex officio* president of the Local Government Board and of the Department of Agriculture and Technical Instruction, and he had a hand in the administration of the Congested Districts Board and the various Educational and Charitable Boards. There were also in Dublin, of course, branches of the major British services such as the Post Office whose headquarters were in London and the Chief Secretary, through the Under-

Secretary acting for him, consulted with these as the occasion demanded. The military and naval establishments were also directed from Britain but the Chief Secretary's Office maintained a close liaison with them and from the day of his arrival – 12 October 1914 – Nathan saw the army chiefs, as well as the heads of the police, practically every day.

CHAPTER FOUR

On his first day in the Castle Nathan reminded himself in his notebook to write to his new chief, Birrell, about a number of points he had found awaiting his attention, the most urgent of them apparently – for he put it first on the list – being the removal, possibly to the Colonies, of Harrell, the second in command of the Dublin Metropolitan Police who, in order that Irish opinion might be placated, had been dismissed from office for 'provocatively' calling out the military to deal with the landing of arms at Howth the previous July. Nathan next proceeded to give himself an introduction to the Irish political scene of which hitherto we may assume he knew comparatively little, and this he did with the help of a précis of information recently prepared by the Crime Special Branch of the Chief Secretary's office. Again he wrote down in his notebook what this taught him. There were five different categories of political organizations in the country : first, the Ulster Volunteer Force numbering 84,000 men; then the Irish Volunteer movement, after which he put an 'R' suggesting that this adhered to John Redmond, the leader of the Irish Parliamentary Party, and comprised 184,000 men with 7,500 rifles. Next he bracketed a Sinn Féin group consisting of the Irish Republican Brotherhood (I.R.B.), Sinn Féin itself, the Ancient Order of Hibernians (Irish-American Alliance) and the Irish National Boy Scouts. In the fourth category he put two bodies – the United Irish League and the Ancient Order of Hibernians (Board of Erin) and to these also, and for the same reason, he gave an 'R'; finally came the Gaelic League which had become a recruiting ground for the I.R.B., although the police did not yet fully realize this.

Nathan also listed the 'advanced' Irish newspapers and marked among them 'for special consideration' – *Sinn Féin, The Irish Volunteer, The Meath Chronicle, Ireland, Fiana* (sic) *Fáil, The*

Irish Worker, which he noted was a weekly edited by Jim Larkin, and *Irish Freedom*. And when he got back from a tour of the Congested Districts, he transcribed from the October police reports a long list of suspects and arranged to bring down District Inspector Blayney from Belfast – a Catholic – to look after them.(*1*) The list included most of the men who were to figure prominently in the history of the next few years – Nathan sometimes added a word or two to fix them in his mind – like Thomas J. Clarke whose shop at 75 Parnell Street was receiving daily attention from the police, Major John McBride, Thomas Ashe ('Gaelic Leaguer'), J. Larkin, James Connolly ('Socialist and pro-German'), Bulmer Hobson, Ernest Blythe (a number in red after his name suggests he had a special file), John T. Kelly ('*Irish Freedom* – Corporation'), Alderman T. Kelly, Arthur Griffith ('*Sinn Féin*'), F. Sheehy Skeffington, C. Colbert (? and National Boy Scouts), P. H. Pearse, John Fitzgibbon, C. Collins ('Clerk, G.P.O.'), E. Kent, W. T. Cosgrave, Countess Markievitz (*sic*) and Pierce Beasley. Special addresses that he noted, apart from T. J. Clarke's shop, were 12 D'Olier Street ('Office of the *Irish Freedom*'); Liberty Hall, Beresford Place; 41 Kildare Street (Office of the Sinn Féin Volunteers); 17 Ormond Quay ('Whelans'); 68 Upper Sackville Street ('Central Council, G.A.A.') and 67 Middle Abbey Street (the office of '*Scissors and Paste*').

Some of the information contained in the list of suspect men and addresses qualified Nathan's first entries. The mention of the Sinn Féin Volunteers shows that what he had first recorded simply as the Irish Volunteer Movement needed to be broken down into the great majority who still followed Redmond, and the two or three thousand who since the end of September had repudiated him because he had declared, without consulting anybody, that the Volunteers should be ready to fight as members of the British forces. The movement thereafter consisted of the Redmondite body known as the National Volunteers, and the Irish Volunteers under the presidency of Eoin MacNeill who were known increasingly to the British and others as Sinn Féiners although the appellation was not entirely accurate. The mention of *Scissors and Paste* draws attention to an omission from Nathan's list of the advanced papers that required special consideration; and, as we shall see, this particular paper occupied a great deal of Nathan's attention. The question of seditious publications generally was actually the first big question he faced in his new office and it figured high on an agenda he prepared for a meeting in London on 20 November with the Minister of War, Lord Kitchener. In his usual methodical way Nathan set out the nature of the publications—newspapers, leaflets and placards; and the heads under which offences could be committed – writing, printing, publishing, exposing for sale and sending through the post. And in the same connection he noted to raise the issue of seditious speeches and proposals for arresting speakers, searching premises and trial by court-martial.

Another question of growing importance was the unlicensed importation of arms into Ireland and possible ways of stopping this traffic. And, finally, he wanted to talk to Kitchener about correspondence with the enemy and invasion. What transpired at the interview we do not know exactly but we can guess its trend from Nathan's general correspondence about these subjects.

The possibility of an invasion of Ireland was, of course, never very far from the minds of the men charged with the defence of these islands. A full year before the outbreak of the 1914–18 war the risks had been reassessed and the Irish departments likely to be concerned had been put on the qui vive.(2) On 2 November 1914, Birrell sent over to Nathan some 'curious telegrams about Roger Casement'. These had come from Christiania, presumably from the British Minister there, and as Birrell put it the next day, they announced the invasion of Ireland by the Germans who, less wise than the Romans, were alleged to be approaching not only Yarmouth but Galway. He awaited developments with immense interest but could hardly believe the news. Still, desperate men did desperate things and Casement, he believed, was *capable de tout*. 'Our navy record', he added, 'is not a bright one in any sea or quarter of the Globe.'(3) Nathan, acknowledging this, supposed the military authorities had been alerted. An invasion of Ireland might appear practicable to the Germans but nothing seemed less likely than that the Irish would rise in support of it. 'In fact,' he wrote, 'it would . . . be a serious blow to the Sinn Féiners if it got to be believed in the country that their activities, especially their publications, were going to lead to a German invasion which they could be forced to join.'

It might be as well if Mr Redmond in one of his speeches suggested that this might happen.(4)

When he discussed invasion possibilities with Kitchener Nathan told him of what he had settled with General Lovick Bransby Friend, the General Officer Commanding the Army in Ireland, whom Arthur Griffith liked to call 'this amiable person'. Kitchener thought that if a landing did occur the Ulster Division should be brought down, for it was apparently assumed that the Germans would make for the south-west coast. Friend considered that this new division was not sufficiently disciplined yet, but Kitchener retorted that they would be as much disciplined as their antagonists by whom he doubtless meant the Volunteers of the South. At the interview Kitchener gave Nathan the benefit of his views on the Irish Parliamentary leaders, Redmond, Dillon and Devlin, whom Birrell repeatedly described as the Irish Trinity.(5) Nathan knew something of these views already as a result of what Dillon had told him at their first meeting and he had sought the help of Lloyd George to try to counteract them. Kitchener had resisted the Irish case that in seeking recruits an appeal to Irish sentiment should take the place in Ireland of the claims to British patriotism made so successfully in Great Britain, and had taken a particularly strong line against having Irish Brigades under Irish officers formed for foreign service, although he had no difficulty in allowing separate Ulster units to be established. He believed in Redmond's loyalty, however, was sceptical of Dillon's and raised his eyebrows when Nathan mentioned Devlin's. Nathan compared Redmond's position to Botha's in South Africa, saw Dillon as Redmond's Smuts, and was impressed by the nationalist leaders' achievements in the recruiting field, particularly Devlin's, despite the hostile propaganda of Sinn Féiners and Larkinites. On the general condition of Ireland, Kitchener was anxious. The country, he told Nathan, was in a state of festering rebellion which must some time come to a head. All the more reason, therefore, for watching Irish contacts with Germany.

Casement was promising his friends a German raid and a Rising in Ireland about Christmas time, so the Government was informed a little later. And around Christmas Day Birrell passed on to Nathan a Foreign Office flimsy which, if only half true, he said, unfolded a tale of incredible folly. But in dealing with

27

Casement, 'with this strain of madness and vanity', they must remember that nothing was impossible. Birrell added that he had reason to believe that Burke Cochrane, the influential American lawyer with whom Casement was in touch, had gone wrong, while the form of John Devoy, the old Clan na Gael man, was well known to them. Kuno Meyer was also one of the Plotters and was pleased because the Irish prisoners of war in Germany had been 'got at'. Birrell speculated about what their enemies contemplated doing. 'It is all very *vague* about numbers and *nationalities*. Are they coming as open *enemies* – to storm our coasts, and seize our Irish Castles or as *secret* agents of the Kaiser? However, we must be ready for either dread contingency! The weather will upset their stomachs if not their plans!'(6)

Nathan lost no time in posting General Friend, and also Sir Neville Francis Fitzgerald Chamberlain, the Inspector General of the Royal Irish Constabulary, who assured him that his force were very much on their toes. He also turned his particular attention to the men understood to be working with Casement, but such information as they were receiving from 'the informer' seemed, in his opinion, to get vaguer instead of more definite. They had to be ready for any eventuality, nevertheless. He cancelled his acceptance of an invitation from his old friend and former political chief, Charlie Hobhouse, to spend Christmas with him in England, for it would be unfortunate, he realized, if after receiving a warning of an invasion he was away from his post at the critical time. Birrell's comment on this was that 'as you are to spend Christmas in Ireland you can do your best to observe the Irish maxim "Be aisy – and if you can't be aisy – be as aisy as you can."(7)

But there was no real basis for this alleged threat of a German invasion in 1914. The suggestion had apparently originated in faked letters Casement had got his man, Adler Christensen, to plant on the British Minister, Findlay, in Christiania during the month of December. One of these authorized Christensen to spend up to $30,000 in chartering a boat and hiring men for the invasion.(8) In handing over other letters, Christensen told Findlay that Casement was receiving almost unlimited money from America with which to charter vessels and engage men. These vessels were to meet Casement on the coast at Schleswig at an early date and were to be used for a transhipment of arms and men at sea.(*9*) To prevent this happening the British fitted out a yacht, the *Sayonara,* and sent it, with naval officers personating Americans, cruising along the West coast of Ireland, shadowed by a coastguard vessel. They paid particular attention to Darrel Figgis who was known to have associated with Casement before the Howth gun-running and who had gone to live on the Island of Achill facing the Atlantic since the summer of 1914. Ostensibly he was devoting himself to writing and to spare-time organization of the Volunteers, but the Authorities suspected him of a more mischievous intent.(*10*) The operation was called off on 9 January 1915, it being then considered that the Irish and Germans had postponed their plans,(*11*) but not before the villages along the Irish coast were placarded with notices to the effect that, in view of a possible attack by the German Fleet, the people were to hold themselves in instant readiness to remove themselves and their chattels inland.(*12*)

We suspect Nathan was not very 'aisy' over the Christmas, for on 28 December he told Friend that he wanted the list of suspects revised to show those who might be a military danger in the event of a raid or armed insurrection and recommended setting up a committee, to meet that very afternoon, consisting of 'Connolly of this office who has a great store of knowledge as to the past movements of these men, and of Major Price, Mr Holmes of the R.I.C. Crime Special Department, and Mr Lowe, Superintendent of the Detective Division of the D.M.P. The regular plotters here seem to be coming together rather more of late and Limerick (John Daly's centre) and Belfast have been visited by some of them.'(*13*) He tightened up the postal censorship system in consultation with Sir Evelyn Murray, the Secretary at the London Headquarters of the Post Office,(*14*) and to the list of persons covered by special warrants he added Denis McCullough (an I.R.B. man) and the Rev. Robert Fullerton, C.C. of St Paul's Presbytery, Belfast.(*15*)

Professor Eoin MacNeill, whose article 'The North Began'(*16*) had brought the Irish Volunteer Movement into existence, had been made a major suspect by the interception of a letter Casement had sent him from Berlin via an address in Holland and that of Mrs Alice Stopford Green in London. This enclosed the German declaration of goodwill towards Ireland, warned against

British intrigue at the Vatican, and asked that the Germans and himself be trusted. 'Tell me all your needs at home,' he told MacNeill, 'viz., rifles, officers, men.'(*17*) Mrs Green was the magnetic widow of J. R. Green, the author of the *Short History of the English People*. She, a child of a Protestant Archdeacon of Meath, had won a reputation as a writer in her own right, had espoused the Home Rule cause, and had given financial and moral support to the new movements that marked the opening years of the century. She had put up about half the money that was required for the Howth gun-running operation. Casement had been an intimate friend since 1904; but she had many acquaintances and friends in other camps as well, among them Birrell, Haldane, Simon and the youthful Winston Churchill. She had also known Nathan for a long time and there had developed a genuine friendship between them which permitted them to speak uninhibitedly about political affairs and to pass to each other their estimations of individuals and parties. They entertained each other in London and Dublin and Mrs Green went occasionally to stay in the Under-Secretary's Lodge in Phoenix Park, taking her niece, Dorothy Stopford, who was a medical student, along with her. One senses that the disappearance of Casement into Germany and the contingent developments in Ireland were not altogether to her liking. And she was naturally disturbed when she heard of the enquiries that were being made about the letter to MacNeill and the covering note to herself sent to her with much love and affection by Casement who described himself romantically, as was his custom, as the Man of the Three Cows whose friends would aid to the uttermost in redeeming the four green fields. She hastened to see Birrell for she feared that harm might befall MacNeill who held a chair in University College in Dublin which received financial aid from the State. But 'I told her', said Birrell, 'that it was not his *Chair* but his *Head* or at least his liberty that was in danger. I think I perplexed her. She laments *his* folly as I do *hers*.'(*18*) 'I don't know how she stands precisely in the hierarchy of treason but I should put her *low down*. . . . Still there *is* or was a *Casement* movement. If there is a D.N.B. within your reach you might turn up Thomas Stuckley – a Knight in Queen Elizabeth's time (some say a bastard of her father's). He meditated an *Irish Rebellion* to put an illegitimate son of the *Pope* on that dangerous and worthless throne, but died in 1578 on the stricken field of Alcaran in Barbary with three kings to keep him company. He was very like Sir Roger Casement – Stuckley was however a Devonian not an Irishman.'(*19*)

Nathan was in London for a long week-end at the end of January 1915. He saw Captain Hall, the Chief of Naval Intelligence, at the Admiralty about the *Sayonara* exploit and raised some question about the activities of 'Darrell Figgis, Journalist, associated with W. B. Yeats'. He lunched with the Viceroy elect, and fixed the details of the swearing-in ceremony. He discussed with Birrell in the Irish Office what to do with the Irish Volunteers and the position of Government servants who were Irish Volunteers, and he saw Mr Redmond. When he got back to Dublin he listed among the things he wanted to talk to General Friend about, the National and Ulster Volunteers, arms for the National Volunteers, *Scissors and Paste,* the R.I.C. and the clearing of coastal counties, by which presumably was meant clearing possible invasion areas of persons likely to be in sympathy with the Germans.(*20*)

The Irish Executive were sick and tired of Lord Aberdeen and were greatly relieved when, having clung like a limpet to office, he finally moved out of Dublin in the middle of February. The identity of his successor had been known since the latter part of December. He was Lord Wimborne, formerly Sir Ivor Churchill Guest, cousin of Winston Churchill, who was elected as a liberal in the 1906 election and accepted a peerage in 1910 to strengthen the government representation in the House of Lords. In 1914 on the outbreak of the war he was appointed to the staff of Lieutenant General Sir Bryan Mahon, then commanding a division at the Curragh, and in a matter of months was offered the Lord Lieutenancy by Asquith. Birrell, who had already established the most confidential relationship with his Under-Secretary, told Nathan that Wimborne was a crude young man without any fine strands of character but if he could keep his temper he did not see why, with his charming wife, he should do so badly and perhaps he might do really well.(*21*) In time, he did rather too well for Birrell's – and Nathan's – liking.

CHAPTER FIVE

Nathan was only in the job a few days when he became aware of the problem of disloyalty in the Civil Service. By and large the Civil Servants in Ireland were as loyal as any others, but there were, he wrote on 5 November 1914, 'a good number of the lower officials in this undesirable organisation, Sinn Féin, which is recognised as undoubtedly pro-German and we shall have, presently, to put some strong check on their increased activity'. He told the Chief Secretary a little later that he was starting to harry them.(*1*) The first men who came under notice were Hugh O'Hehir and Michael Lynch, clerks in the Irish Land Commission, who were reported by the police to be 'in communication with Sinn Féin authorities'. He wrote to the Land Commission about them, and to the Revenue Authorities suggesting a transfer to a station in England for Mr Peter Moore 'where his work would not be prejudicially affected by the contagion of local excitement'. He had a note from Sir John G. Barton, the Commissioner of Valuation, about his Sinn Féin clerk, and told him he had asked the Treasury to remove him. Simultaneously he was giving attention to some of the undesirables in the Post Office. 'The name of Patrick O'Keefe', he told Norway, 'appears on today's "suspect" list as visiting the Sinn Féin office. The name was familiar and you may have mentioned it to me. Will you please tell me about him and see that he does not go on any duty that might make him a danger to public safety.' Then there was Cornelius Collins, a clerk in the Parcels Post in Amiens Street. The R.I.C. were watching him but Nathan wished to know all about him and particularly about the circumstances of his going to Limerick. Norway was not helpful: he took Collins off the handling of telegrams where he might have been harmful(2) but he raised a general question which Nathan brusquely told him he was not prepared to admit.

32

Was Norway contending that it was no affair of government departments that their servants should openly be connected with societies and persons whose avowed intention it was to injure the government, so long as these persons were not individually guilty of offences against the public peace? He well understood Norway's difficulties and his dislike of taking action unless some definite Post Office rule was infringed, but could not a Post Office circular be devised which would forbid such connections? In time of war, at any rate, when loyalty of service must be beyond suspicion such an intimation could scarcely be regarded as unduly oppressive. And he asked Norway 'to sketch out a draft' which they could discuss together. Norway apparently made some suggestions of a disciplinary character but, being apparently doubtful as to whether his people in London would approve of them, he suggested to Nathan that he might consult his friend, Hobhouse, who was then the Postmaster General and this Nathan did. He did so while O'Keefe was being reported by the police to be marching about in uniform with the Sinn Féin Volunteers.

In raising the case of the 'troublesome' Cornelius Collins, Nathan explained to Hobhouse that he was only one of many suspects and he enclosed a list for inspection. 'For some reason which I am unable to fathom,' he wrote, 'a large proportion of the people treasonable to England (patriotic to Ireland, they would put it) are to be found in the lower ranks of the government service and in this respect the Post Office has a bad pre-eminence. In ordinary times the machinations of these people are not of so much importance as now when the aims of the Associations to which they belong – avowedly to stop recruiting and embarrass the government by every means in their power – can to some extent be carried out.

'This particular man Collins was brought to notice by your predecessor in . . . June 1911 as having been actively engaged in the Sinn Féin organisation and in an anti-Coronation demonstration. He was then and is still living in the house of one of the most active of the suspects—John McDermott. On 21st of last month, being on leave, he went to Limerick. His visit synchronised with that of a revolutionary – T. J. Clarke – who is an ex-convict, and Collins stayed at the house of another revolutionary – John Daly – also an ex-convict.

33

'In addition to Collins and these two ex-convicts, a fourth man took part in these deliberations, a man of the name of Monteith, who was recently dismissed from the Ordnance Stores in Dublin on suspicion of being engaged in treasonable practices and ordered away from his post by the military authorities. While it would be difficult to take criminal or court-martial proceedings against Collins for belonging to a revolutionary organisation and associating closely with its leaders, these things do undoubtedly make him a most undesirable public servant and I should be glad if you can fit in with any suggestions Norway may make for dealing with him severely.'(3) When he was calling off his Christmas visit on account of the Casement scare, Nathan mentioned the difficulties the Post Office was having with the Service Associations in regard to it. The general feeling, however, in which he said Redmond and Dillon joined, was that they could not at this time have in the service persons belonging to organizations that were avowedly hostile to the government. Such steps as they had already taken to get rid of them were having a wholesome effect.(4)

Hobhouse, however, was not going to pull the chestnuts out of the fire for the Civil and Military Authorities in Ireland. The constabulary evidence he considered vague and loose. He was prepared to take the strongest disciplinary measures against any Postal officer who was really disloyal, but he would have to get 'good evidence' to justify his action.(5) Nathan, dissatisfied, got Birrell to raise the matter in the Cabinet(6) and there obtained approval for a letter he had drafted warning civil servants that dismissal would follow continued membership of the Irish Volunteers. The first person to be dismissed was Miss Elizabeth N. Somers of Dalkey 'on suspicion of being connected with disloyal agencies'. She had acted in a manner prejudicial to recruiting and thus to the successful termination of the war. 'I think', he said, 'it will be time enough for the Postmaster General (or the Irish Minister for Posts and Telegraphs) to reconsider the case when that termination has been reached and when what Miss Somers terms indiscretions are fraught with less serious danger to this country and to the realization of its aspirations.' Despite this big talk, however, Nathan was trying a few months later to get Miss Somers a job somewhere else.

On the list of suspects was Austin Stack, the Income Tax

Collector for Dingle and Cahirciveen whom the police described as 'an advanced G.A.A. man and pro-German' who in 1910 had torn down and burned a photograph of King Edward. And Norway was horrified to find that two of his own staff, Mahon and McCrossan of Strabane, had recently been reported as having joined the I.R.B. (the Irish Republican Brotherhood) which was a continuation of the Fenian movement of the 1860s. 'Is it really a fact,' he asked Nathan, 'that that sinister organization, a far more dangerous body than Sinn Féin, has come to life again? Perhaps it never died absolutely. But if new life has been breathed into the old organization, the fact would be one of gravity, according to my information and would justify sharp and drastic steps. . . .' Nathan replied that the I.R.B. was indeed alive, and that membership of it betokened sympathy with the most advanced section of the Sinn Féiners. As an effective independent organization, however, it had little current importance though circles of it were still occasionally held, mostly in the North of Ireland. At one time its membership was estimated at nearly 40,000, but it could not now exceed 1,000. The fact that Mahon and McCrossan had recently joined the I.R.B. might be taken as indicative of their being ready for any mischief, not involving great criminality, that might develop.(7) Another Post Office man more capable immediately of mischief was Michael Cremin who went to Cork for his Christmas holidays in 1915 with fifteen rifles and fifty revolvers.

The Military shared the doubts of the police about the Post Office. Troops were being embarked at many points, and it was of great importance that details of the units involved should not leak out. This brought under their notice P. S. Hegarty, the Postmaster of Queenstown, a port at which there were many secret goings-on. A high officer called on Norway to say that Hegarty must not remain at Queenstown, or indeed in Ireland. Norway asked why, seeing that the man's official reputation was high, and that he held the complete confidence of the London head office, where he had worked for years. The answer was guarded, but explicit : Hegarty was known to have been in very recent communication with the German Ambassador! Thoroughly convinced, Norway gave an assurance that he would act at once and the officer left, muttering that in wartime traitors were shot. So Hegarty was transferred to Welshpool in Montgomeryshire where he remained throughout the war, coming no more under official notice. 'But', Norway wrote years later, 'I may say if only to show . . . how just were the unproved suspicions of the Military Intelligence, that Hegarty has now written a book (*The Victory of Sinn Féin*) in which he reveals the fact that even when he was earning golden opinions in the secretariat he was already not only a secret member of the Irish Republican Brotherhood, but one of its chief directors, and that he continued to direct it actively from Welshpool. Of this I had not the least inkling.'(*8*)

Military Intelligence also asked Norway to take John Hegarty, a brother of the Postmaster of Queenstown, out of the Cork Post Office where he was employed as a sorter. The evidence pointed clearly enough to association with dangerous and disloyal men, but established no fact which could be said to justify punishment. Thus the case could only be met by transfer to an equivalent position out of Ireland. Hegarty would not go to England, however, and was dismissed for disobedience. Some weeks later anti-recruiting notices were found posted up in different parts of County Wexford which were believed to be in his handwriting, and a warrant was issued for his arrest. He was discovered in bed in Enniscorthy with a man named James Bolger and the police found in the room a quantity of seditious notices and pamphlets, and a paper parcel containing nineteen sticks of dynamite and some ·303 cartridges. Hegarty and Bolger were removed to Arbour Hill Barracks while the government pondered over the prosecution. When they were arrested, the Defence of the Realm Regulations provided for trial by court-martial only, but an amending Bill was before Parliament so action was deferred. In the House of Lords an amendment was introduced into the Bill on the initiative of Lord Parmoor which gave accused persons the right to elect to be tried by judge and jury, and this was a provision of which the Sinn Féiners made full use. Juries could usually be relied on to throw out prosecutions, not because they liked the accused but because the Attorney General was the prosecutor. It was an old tradition hard to break to be 'agin the government'. Hegarty, when first arraigned on the charge of possessing dynamite, was defended by Tim Healy who pressed with great ingenuity the point that no evidence existed to show what the prisoner had intended to do with the dynamite. The jury was impressed and acquitted him. As Hegarty left the Court he was re-arrested on the seditious literature charge. Again Healy defended him and this time induced the jury to disagree. A third trial followed, and on this occasion Healy secured an acquittal and an end to the proceedings.(9)

CHAPTER SIX

When together they first faced the problem of the seditious press, Birrell confessed how glad he was that Nathan's judgement was now available to him. He had got so into the habit 'of letting the Pig cut its own throat', he said, and had so deep-rooted a contempt for most kinds of newspapers that his judgement was warped. Nathan, new to Ireland, was alarmed by the content and tone of the advanced papers but he wanted to discover the mind of the Irish Party in relation to them, for he recognized that it would be wrong to take any action that would embarrass the leaders of the large loyal majority of Nationalist Ireland. He thought that Birrell might get Redmond's view as to whether the time had not come for action; he would approach Redmond himself were it not that the Irish leader might decline to commit himself to one he knew so slightly. 'You will remember,' Nathan told Birrell, 'that Mr Dillon spoke definitely against such action (as had been suggested) but matters have developed since. The campaign has become more violent instead of tending to die down as we had hoped it would and the increased newspaper activity indicates plentiful funds which must come from a foreign source.' (A circular letter which was picked up a few weeks later modified the view that large sums of money were being forwarded to the Revolutionaries. Such money as they had been getting from the States had been spent on arms.) At the same time he expressed doubt as to whether action against the press, even if it succeeded in totally suppressing anti-recruiting publications, would result in many more men joining the forces. But by not attempting to control sedition they were weakening the country militarily and making its future government more difficult. It was from this aspect that Redmond's views were important. If he thought that action would not injure the Irish Parliamentary Party Nathan would be in favour of the military taking steps under D.O.R.A. to stop the issue of the violent papers. How violent they were would be seen from the issues of the *Irish Volunteer* and *Ireland* that he posted to Birrell (3 November 1914). Birrell told him that so far as Dillon was concerned he might take it that whatever appeared in the *Freeman's Journal* represented his view, and the *Freeman* was averse to any immediate proceedings against the Sinn Féin newspapers, if newspapers they could be called. It did not follow, however, that Redmond agreed with Dillon, so that they would have to make up their own minds (4 November 1914). Before doing this, Nathan lunched with Devlin who spoke very definitely – evidently after consultation with Dillon – against suppressing the introduction of arms by them. He used the arguments, Nathan reported, with which the Government were familiar, that the Sinn Féiners were a small minority, that Irishmen were not affected by the stuff that appeared in the seditious press, and that it would be playing into their hands to make martyrs of them.

Nathan saw more of John Dillon than of any other member of the Irish Party. This was understandable because Dillon, besides being John Redmond's principal lieutenant, was more frequently in Ireland and had a town house in Dublin within a mile or so of the Castle. The first of these meetings took place on the evening of 26 November 1914, in the quiet of W. F. Bailey's house in Earlsfort Terrace that George Moore recalls in the closing lines of his trilogy *Hail and Farewell*. Bailey, in addition to being a Land Commissioner, was a trustee of the Abbey Theatre, a governor of the National Gallery and other things besides, and the choice of his house was in accordance with the almost pathological objection of the Irish leaders to meetings within the Castle walls or in the official residences in the Phoenix Park or indeed in any public place. It was too soon for that, in their view, even with Home Rule in the offing.

Dillon had asked for this talk, for he wanted to advise the Government to leave the seditious papers alone. That very day there had been articles in the *Freeman's Journal* and the *Irish News* on these lines, but Nathan was determined to oppose any concession. Although less than two months in Ireland he had told Birrell that he was already tired of hearing the Sinn Féiners called 'an insignificant minority'. They were not an insignificant

39

minority and it was not true to say that they had no influence. He was a little inclined to think that the Nationalist leaders would like to see action taken so long as they did not appear to be associated with it. He duly gave Birrell an account of this meeting with Dillon 'though', he said, 'there is little in it beyond the expression of which you are already cognisant'. Dillon, as he anticipated, insisted that it was a mistake to take too much notice of Sinn Féin activities and would not listen to Nathan when he quoted Froude to the effect that in a state of war the *salus populi* overrode all other considerations and that the maxims and laws of calmer periods had to be suspended.

Nathan later sent Dillon the Froude reference(*1*), and received a spirited reply. The particular principle laid down by Froude, Dillon told him, only applied to normal countries while Ireland's situation was almost unique. He asked Nathan to read Dean Swift who was a much sounder authority on all things Irish. In the face of complicated obstacles which it would take Nathan years of study to appreciate, the Irish Party had been endeavouring to effect a genuine reconciliation between two peoples who for centuries had detested each other and inflicted terrible injuries on each other. The outbreak of the war, following on the enactment of Home Rule, had created a position of terrible difficulty and of embarrassment for the Irish Party. Up to quite recently the War Office had done nothing but add to the difficulties. 'Yet,' he said, 'we have retained the confidence and the membership of about twenty to one of the Nationalists of Ireland, and secured their goodwill to England in the war. And according to my information we have completely paralyzed the attempts of the Germans to secure the co-operation of the Irish in America in influencing American opinion against England. I do *not* believe that the Sinn Féiners and pro-Germans are making any headway against us in Ireland.' But the suppression of 'those scurrilous rags' might have an evil influence on the whole situation and raise fresh obstacles in the path of recruiting from the ranks of Irish Nationalists.

Birrell saw this letter and observed that 'John Dillon's lucubrations are always cast in the same mould but are never without some *thought* in them, an unusual contribution from National or indeed any other *Irish* source. I don't myself *anticipate* great *advantage* from raiding the Press – the fatal disease is there, deep buried in certain Irishmen and women – Casements, Greens, Fords, Devoys, Wolfe Tones and so on to Rory O'Moore. But *action* is forced upon us by the feeling in England and the anti-Home Rule feeling in Ireland. I mean the *Unionist* anti-Home Rule feeling, and also by the danger of a real street row and sham rebellion in Dublin. I agree with you in thinking that the Parliamentary Party are holding themselves free to watch what happens—if it succeeds, they will be able to say they were quite willing—if it fails they can shrug their shoulders and say Dublin Castle are at the old game!'

On 30 November Nathan communicated the Government's decision to Dillon. They were going 'to stop the diffusion of printed and verbal statements intended to create disaffection among the troops and the civilian population of Ireland'. Though the ultimate responsibility did not rest mainly on himself he did not wish to disclaim his share of it. He recognized all the difficulties that must follow any coercive measure and he had personally a strong dislike to such measures, but there were worse evils, and the growing lawlessness that was encouraged by certain papers and represented by the armed mobs which were now taking possession of parts of Irish cities had to be checked. Armed mobs were Nathan's description of the Irish Volunteers; they assembled, he continued, to hear hatred-reviving speeches that no government could allow at that time of national peril and paramountcy of military interests. They could hardly stop the speeches which were heard by a few hundred persons and do nothing to the papers that were seen by many thousands. 'From my short experience in this country,' he added, 'I believe Irishmen *are* affected by what they hear and read probably more than more phlegmatic peoples. When you and Mr Redmond hold anti-hatred meetings in the country I am quite sure you pull out people from the Sinn Féin ranks. But the Sinn Féin leaders—the less prominent as well as the more prominent—are very active; they seem always on the move and, as far as I can judge from the reports I receive, to be constantly getting new recruits. Their cleverly worded and insidiously scattered papers spread all over the country, and in the distribution of leaflets they and their American allies have the field practically to themselves. I sometimes wish there had been a stronger newspaper and leaflet "reconciliation" campaign and wonder whether the strength of the hatred party has not been under-estimated by the regular press in Ireland. I lay no special stress on the recruiting aspect of the question because I am doubtful whether this is much affected by the Sinn Féin Movement . . . I shall be very glad if you will tell me the further measures which you think the War Office should still adopt in this matter so that I may add my advocacy of these to yours.' And he ended by declaring his distress that Dillon should think that the action to be taken to prevent the spread of disaffection would increase the already great difficulties of the Irish Party. 'I need not say that if by the methods of our action against the papers we could obviate this to any extent I would greatly appreciate any suggestions you would make. . . .'

Nathan, having got the necessary authority, pushed ahead with the preparation of comprehensive regulations under D.O.R.A. including power to seize and destroy printing plants, and on 2 December he sent a message to Birrell indicating that speedy action had followed. 'Irish Freedom', he wrote, 'appeared last night. It was a very bad number, and the police have been seizing it today.' But Birrell, while committed to the policy, continued to be unenthusiastic about it. When the case of *Scissors and Paste* was brought to his notice he declared that it was not worth powder and shot; it contained nothing in the least likely to do anybody harm. The military, however, insisted on action and Nathan pressed Birrell to agree. What he had in mind was to confiscate an issue as well as Mr Mahon's previously threatened printing press, when the next bad number appeared. The *Irish Volunteer*, he said, had become very mild since a warning was given to the printers. Birrell gave in. 'I am not going to make a fuss . . .' he replied. 'No, I could wish the War Office a foeman more worthy of their thunderbolts.' He would personally have liked to include in the act of suppression *The Spectator* and one or two other English papers that were creating a reaction against the war which might become serious. They had not to wait long for the next bad number of *Scissors and Paste*; on 26 January Nathan was telling Birrell that General Friend had written to the War Office for permission to put the paper out of circulation.

On the other hand, Birrell had no illusions about where the importation of arms was leading them. What was happening was most dangerous and alarming. And to make things worse the control over the Redmondite volunteers had slackened so much that they were allowing the other fellows to steal their rifles. Colonel Maurice Moore was invited to the Castle to tell him that he must enquire into the custody of his arms all over the country and issue proper instructions regarding them, and on another occasion Nathan told Redmond of a report that Dr McCartan of Gortin, Father Coyle of Fintona and Father O'Daly of Clogher were trying to buy rifles stored for the National Volunteers in Omagh. 'I suggest', he said, 'that it might be advisable to ascertain that the persons who are in charge of these rifles for you are strictly reliable.'(2) Birrell agreed that it was certain that Sinn Féin could be crushed at any time by soldiers, but if armed it would only be after considerable loss of life and bloodshed which at that time of foreign war was specially to be deprecated. He, therefore, endorsed Nathan's suggested prohibition; if it involved legislation, it ought to be obtained at once.

Both Birrell and Nathan were subjected to pressure not only from the Nationalists but from the opposing Unionist camp. The Nationalists continued to declare their opposition to the suppression of the so-called seditious press, although Nathan suspected that they spoke increasingly with their tongues in their cheeks. The Unionists, on the other hand, wanted strong action against the papers and Nathan was the recipient of representations from a number of them. Among the first to write to him in a friendly way was Lord Selbourne. He was very glad that Nathan, for whom he had a great regard, was handling this business himself, and not leaving it all to the military. As for the others—'I do not think that Birrell has got any instincts of government at all, and as for dear Aberdeen!'(3)

About this time Nathan prepared for the Earl of Midleton an account of the position in an effort to correct the thinking of the Southern Irish Unionists of whom he was the leader. He strongly suggested to him that by expressing alarm in public about the growth of the Irish Volunteer movement he was unconsciously doing a great deal to advertise the efforts of a revolutionary group whom he believed were insignificant and decreasing in number although vocal out of proportion to their strength. He sent a copy of his paper to Walter Long, when he

43

wrote transmitting criticism of Government policy that had been formulated by one of his associates. Before dealing with specific points Nathan claimed that not merely had he access to more extensive sources of information, which was undoubtedly true, but that he was as free as any man from political bias and had personal friends in all parties, which was also true but not demonstrably so. He gave an example of this when he came to deal with *The Irish Volunteer* which it was alleged continued to print grossly seditious articles that called for punitive action. This he denied and he sent Long a copy of the last number issued of the paper. As might be expected, however, Long, having read the paper 'carefully and more than once', confessed that he was much distressed to find that Nathan did not consider the publication injurious and one that ought to be stopped. He found it difficult to understand why practices which would not be tolerated on the English side of the Channel were allowed in Ireland and he warned Nathan to expect an unpleasant re-action in the House of Commons from his political associates including men of moderate and statesmanlike view. 'We are fighting for our lives, we have a terrible task before us, we want every man we can get, and above all, we want absolutely united action, and the feeling is I think very strong that the time has come when everybody has to be taught that no treasonable language, no attempt to interfere with recruiting, no language hostile to the Cause of the Empire, will be tolerated. Believe me, I have great sympathy with Redmond . . . but it is quite evident from the articles in the *Irish Volunteer* that the best way to help him is to let these traitors know that their evil practices will be suppressed . . .' (3 January 1915).

Nathan replied that the only fact that Long's informant had got right was that the Sinn Féiners were in a minority *vis-à-vis* Redmond's volunteers; they represented about one-sixteenth. But he was quite wrong in saying that they had a vast superiority in rifles; they had less than one-sixth. He was likewise only partially right in thinking that the anti-German sentiment of the Redmondite volunteers had not as yet found expression in any desire to enlist in the British Army. In the previous month (October 1914) more Redmondite than Ulster Volunteers had joined. It was true that they had come mostly from the industrial north; and Long's correspondent was generally right in the reasons he gave why the peasant people in agricultural Ireland were slow to enlist. But Nathan assured Long that all his friend's points, including the possibility of a German raid on the West Coast, were constantly in his mind. He was using such poor intelligence as he had for dealing with them in the way he believed would best prevent harm arising from the ill-will towards England undoubtedly borne by a section of the Irish people (not extinguishable by suppression of papers and persons) and which would also extend and consolidate the loyalty of the many Nationalists who were now in sympathy with the Empire (26 December 1914). He maintained this contact with Long and through him reached out to some of the moderates among the Unionists. This helped to prepare a visit he paid to Belfast in April 1915 which he told Long he enjoyed very much, though there was another side to the picture. 'I am not surprised to learn,' Long told him on his return, 'that you came away feeling rather hopeless for the future, and I confess I don't see any chance myself of an early decease of these old but well-founded prejudices. The good thing to remember is that their foundation is fact and not imagination, and therefore they will be very difficult to remove. . . .'(4)

Nathan advised Redmond and Dillon in mid-February of his discussions with Long, but this was incidental in an interview intended to be the first of a number, which Nathan arranged after first obtaining the approval of the Prime Minister(4a), in order to give the Nationalist leaders an opportunity of discussing the machinery of Irish government in anticipation of their taking over. They apparently had a good deal to learn for, 'it was amusing how Redmond admitted – with perfect truth as well as candour – his entire ignorance of Irish government'.(5) Subsequently Nathan sent the two Irishmen a revised list of departments and their functions, with particulars of the statutory adaptations that would be required, and he asked the various heads of the Irish Departments confidentially to prepare memoranda regarding the position they would find themselves in under the Government of Ireland Act, 1914. He also got Headlam, the Treasury Remembrancer, to advise regarding suitable staff for a Department of Finance, and gave his own views regarding the functions of such a department.

Following these moves Nathan and Dillon communicated frequently with each other and met occasionally – outside the Castle. 'I spent a couple of hours on Saturday afternoon with Mr Dillon,' Nathan told Birrell on 7 December. 'Very pleasant company . . .' On 26 January 1915 'Mr Dillon wrote last week that he wanted to see me at North Great George's Street (Dillon's Dublin house) on Friday and Mr Devlin at Gardiner's Row on Saturday. The self-denying principle that prevents these gentlemen coming to the Castle has its troublesome side but on the whole I like seeing them, especially Dillon . . .' In March Redmond and Dillon agreed to attend an early morning meeting in the Under-Secretary's Lodge but sidestepped an invitation to breakfast there. Nathan usually consulted Dillon about appointments as, for instance, that of William Magennis to fill a vacancy on the Board of Education,(6) and this was regarded by Dillon as a right and proper thing in the circumstances, something they expected a government should do that was about to divest itself of jurisdiction.

At their first meeting in Bailey's house Nathan had tried to get from Dillon 'the reasons for the faith that was in him with regard to Murphy versus Quinn'. These men were being considered for the vacant Assistant Commissionership of the D.M.P. and the Irish Party had expressed an interest in the filling of the position. Both men were Catholics and Dillon appeared to have a preference for Murphy. Quinn got the job, however, because Nathan's police advisers believed he was the better of the two, but they would have preferred another person altogether, Superintendent Lowe of the Detective Division who was a Protestant, and would have so recommended were it not that they recognised that 'the weaker alternative might be the wiser one at the present time'.(7) Nathan did not need to be told by his staff that 'the unfortunate circumstances' of the country were against such an appointment. He knew well, as Dillon bluntly told him, that 'the appointment of an Ulster Protestant at this juncture would undoubtedly be taken as a declaration of war'.(8) The views of the Irish Party did not count for so much, however, when the Tories joined Asquith in a coalition.

Nathan would have preferred the principle of the best man for the job regardless of religion but he recognized the need for a modification of this in Irish circumstances. There were some appointments to Boards that traditionally were appointed to

Protestants and Catholics, and in this as in other matters he took his cue from Birrell who, though he personally rather preferred Catholics to Protestants was wary of Catholics who were known in Ireland as being of the 'Castle' variety. Of one of these, a lawyer who was trying to advance his claims to preferment as a Nationalist, Birrell burst out in one of his intimate notes to Nathan : 'I am surprised to hear that ——, K.C., is a Nationalist; nobody would call him one. He is a Catholic and a trimmer and I would prefer almost anybody else.'(9) But Birrell could be grossly inconsistent if it suited his book. When O'Dea, the Catholic Bishop of Galway, was suggested for membership of the Congested Districts Board he described him (10) as 'a good rigid prelate who puts the Church first and Ireland a good second. He *lectures* his *flock* who don't appear to attach much importance to what he says. He can't be got and never will be got to see the English or Treasury point of view about anything. With him Ireland is the Pope's back garden. Still he does know many of the aspects of the case . . . I don't think it would be a wise appointment *just now* when we most particularly need a man who understands England and English sentiment.'(11) And of the Viceroy and Vicereine who had sponsored his recommendation he commented that 'the Aberdeens are unfortunate in all their proceedings and undertakings'; it had even been reported that they had had a German spy, a Miss Garland, staying with them.(12)

Birrell was accustomed to express himself thus uninhibitedly to Nathan about personalities. When he got the Irish proposals for the New Year (1915) Honours List he struck out as 'impossible' the name of T. P. Gill, the ex-Nationalist M.P. who had become Secretary of the Department of Agriculture and Technical Instruction; he was 'a scribbler and a humbug, who has already had too much pudding'. Starkie, the Commissioner of Education, on the other hand, was certainly entitled to a knighthood 'if he was ass enough to want one'.(13) In an entirely different context he referred to another celebrity and said he did not know and probably never would know what Redmond really thought of him. 'He is a *literary* gent – with a congenital thirst, and as vain as he is thirsty, but I think he is an honest man.'(14)

Dillon approached Nathan sometimes in individual cases. One of these was a man who was disappointed when Norway was

47

made Secretary of the G.P.O. in 1912 and who believed that, without giving a pledge, Mr Herbert Samuel, the Postmaster General, had promised him the succession at the end of two years. In a strictly confidential letter, Dillon said that 'We all understood that an arrangement to that effect had been come to' but that 'Mr Hobhouse (Samuel's successor), without consulting us or talking the matter over with us extended Mr Norway's appointment for two years. This appeared to us to be a breach of the understanding. I have some reason to believe that Mr Norway is anxious to get back to London, and that an attempt may now be made to appoint another man in Norway's place for the balance of the two years—or even permanently. Are you', he enquired, 'on such terms with Mr Hobhouse as would make it possible for you to take up this matter with him?'(15) Hobhouse had already been approached by 'all sorts of people', including Redmond, Dillon and Devlin, and gave Nathan his views on the subject. The man Dillon had spoken to him about was, he said, 'a very able man, but he is not above trying to pull wires on his own behalf. I have made quite clear to both Redmond and Dillon what the position with regard to Norway is. The latter will stay in his present appointment until the Home Rule government comes in and then he will be abolished; that may be a year hence or two years or three years. We do not want him back in the G.P.O. and he will not be sorry to obtain abolition terms. But I have not, and I will not, commit myself as to ——'s appointment, and neither Dillon nor anyone else has any right to say that Samuel in any way prevented me from following my own policy in this respect. I am not quite sure whether it might not be well to give Mr —— a strong hint, should the opportunity occur, that he will hurt and not forward his prospect of obtaining the secretaryship by thus trying to pull wires in his favour; but you will know best whether such a course or suggestion is either possible or judicious'. It need hardly be said that this suggestion was not acted on. Dillon was simply told that 'Norway will stay in his present appointment until the Home Rule Government comes in and then will be abolished. I fear I cannot usefully take any further steps in the matter. There is at any rate no intention to appoint another man in Norway's place.'(16)

Nathan was in London every few months for official talks

and he always noted in his diary whether the crossing of the Irish Sea was smooth or rough, and whether any German submarines were known to be about; that was a factor that made the easiest passage unpleasant. He occasionally saw Lloyd George, whose protegé he was, and who had plans for taking him away from Ireland for more responsible duties: War Finance and the Secretaryship of the Ministry of Munitions were both mentioned. On these visits he usually saw the Asquiths at Number 10 Downing Street, and sometimes Violet Asquith came over to Dublin. She was there with Lady Scott, the widow of the Arctic explorer, towards the end of April 1915 and dined in the Under Secretary's Lodge, in a company that included Lady Fingall, the Hannays, Bailey and the Horace Plunketts, on the night that the news of the death of her great friend Rupert Brooke was broken to her. She returned to London the following day and Nathan marked the painful episode by inserting in his diary at that point Brooke's famous poem *The Soldier*:

If I should die, think only this of me
That there's some corner of a foreign field that is for ever
England.

Lady Scott stayed on, and Nathan took her to the Abbey to see *Maurice Harte* and *Blanco Posnet*. The acting was 'fine in a sad ill-constructed play and a noisy well-ending one'. Afterwards they went to a theatrical party in the Bailey restaurant. Nathan talked to the much lionized AE whom Lady Scott was keen on going bathing with before breakfast, and Sara Algood and 'Mr Kerrigan' recited for 'a pleasant artistic crowd'.(*17*)

49

CHAPTER SEVEN

While Dillon usually met Nathan, Redmond did his business mainly with the Chief Secretary for whom he had a high regard. This was facilitated, of course, by the fact that Redmond, like Birrell, spent so much time in London. The beginnings of an estrangement between Redmond and Dillon were to be seen by the end of 1914. Dillon had never been happy about Redmond's pledge at the declaration of the war, and he was critical of Redmond later for not taking a stronger line against the Government who had allowed the Army chiefs to mismanage the recruiting campaign in Ireland, going so far even as to refuse a commission to Redmond's son who later distinguished himself for gallantry. And when Redmond, with the idea of using the Volunteers as an auxiliary military force for coastal defence, propounded a scheme of which the Prime Minister approved, Lord Kitchener promptly knifed it. He did not trust the Southern Irish at all; though as time passed he could distinguish, as indeed many other Englishmen did, between Redmond and the other Nationalist leaders. Redmond was genuinely anxious to see Ireland giving as many recruits as possible to the new armies. He believed in the cause for which he thought the War was being fought, and believed also that loyalty, indicated by high recruiting figures, would pay dividends after the war.

When a Coalition government was being formed in May 1915 in the hope of securing a better output of munitions and a more vigorous prosecution of the war, Redmond was invited to become a member but refused. He asked, however, that the introduction of Unionists, including Carson and Long, should not be made an excuse for displacing Birrell and Nathan. Birrell, he asked, should be given a free hand to carry on the government of Ireland with the same officials, and when he heard that this was intended, he told Birrell that it was the only bright feature in the situation. Birrell was depressed however. He would have liked to relinquish office; he thought the job he was doing was 'odious and hateful'; and that the award of influential rank to the most violent protagonists of Unionism seemed to make an end of Home Rule. He was also afraid of conscription or compulsory registration which '*quo ad* Ireland' was just as bad. 'We may escape *shipwreck* and *disturbances* on a big scale in Ireland,' he wrote, 'I pray it may be so. Ireland is, I am sure, in a rotten state – ripe for a row, without leadership.'(*1*)

Writing of the Coalition which he abhorred, Birrell told Haldane, who had been displaced from the Lord Chancellorship to make room for a Tory, that he did not really know how it had happened, 'but I know', he said 'that it is *horrible* and reflects infinite discredit upon the men with whom I am, sorely against my will, condemned to sit. It is all so vulgar, wretched and absurd that I try to muffle it up like the remnants of a bad dream. Nothing now matters, in one sense, except the war and *winning* it, if it is won, and it won't be this New Cabinet that did it. I see nothing immediately in front of us in the *House of Commons* but bad temper, danger and difficulty. The Lobbies and the Whips will have plenty to keep them at work. My particular *team* are furious over *Carson* and now *Campbell*. With compulsory service *in the offing* we may yet see Ireland in rebellion. However, I write not to *disclose* my personal sorrows, anxieties and frustrations but to express my abiding love, affection and esteem for you and my sense of *shame*.'(*1a*)

The recruiting campaign had continued to yield good results on into 1915 despite the irreparable mischief caused by stupidity and neglect, but it now began to flag following the consternation spread by the reports of the Suvla Bay landing,(*2*) and the new Viceroy called a recruiting conference at the Viceregal Lodge which Redmond attended. This led to the disbandment of recruiting committees and the appointment, at Redmond's suggestion, of the Viceroy himself as Director of Recruiting. In this new capacity Wimborne travelled in different parts of the country and was agreeably surprised by the reception he received. Indeed, he formed the opinion that the Sinn Féiners were quantitatively negligible and that a considerable reduction in the police force was quite feasible, but Nathan was not convinced that Viceregal visits gave a good idea of the state of the country.(3) Wimborne was not easily put off, however. He made his opinions known in other quarters so that the untouchable Royal Irish Constabulary, traditionally the backbone of English occupation in Ireland, came under heavy fire as a possible source of recruiting. 'Yesterday afternoon,' Birrell told Nathan on 30 September, 'Redmond and I had a long and very friendly talk with Kitchener of Khartoum at the War Office about Irish recruiting etc. When we meet I will tell you all about it. But I hadn't realized (as I might have) that both these Pundits would lead a heavy *assault* upon me on the subject of the R.I.C. Lord Kitchener exhibited an *animation* to which I was a stranger and put the Question – how many can you spare *now*? Redmond would have it (knowing very little about it) that 2,000 could go – nobody would miss them. The *mice* all agree the *cats* may go to the Front.'

For Birrell, as much as anybody else, recruiting remained the top priority, but in order to facilitate it, it was important that the home atmosphere should be kept as sweet as possible. For this reason he directed Nathan to let out some Sinn Féin prisoners when a good time came, and only to re-arrest them if they showed themselves *anti-recruiters,* and not merely pro-Irish Volunteers. To prosecute them in public for this, he believed, would be popular.

The Sinn Féiners, as they were generally called, although still a small minority, were making progress. Their Volunteer force grew, and became more efficient, while their propaganda against having anything to do with the British Army fell on ears to which the War, allegedly being fought for small nationalities, no longer made a romantic appeal. 'Remember Belgium is good— for Belgians,' said the *Spark*, 'the cry, "Remember Ireland" is sound sense for Irishmen.' And the possibility of conscription helped them further although the Nationalists were as much opposed to this as anybody. In other ways, too, the movement gained increased notoriety. Men were sentenced to terms of imprisonment for the possession of explosives and for making anti-recruiting speeches. Expulsion orders against Volunteer officers and instructors were ignored and the men concerned went to jail. The seditious papers were as provocative as ever, money was openly collected for the purchase of arms, public meetings were held and fiery speeches delivered, and drilling with and without arms was widespread. But what gave the greatest fillip was the funeral of the old Fenian, Jeremiah O'Donovan Rossa. His body was brought from the United States and an enormous multitude, many of them in uniform, followed the coffin to Glasnevin cemetery and listened to an impassioned speech from P. H. Pearse who, while one of Nathan's suspects, had, quite unknown to him, risen to an eminent position in the Irish Revolutionary Movement and was shortly to become Commander in Chief of the Army of the Irish Republic and President of its Provisional Government. His peroration described Nathan and his colleagues as fools who thought they had pacified Ireland, not understanding that Ireland unfree would never be at peace. But this was probably lost on the Castle authorities who, once more in order to avoid provocation, had given instructions that there were to be no note-takers at the graveside.(4)

In advance of the funeral, Nathan realized that the occasion would be used for a demonstration. He wrote to Dillon : 'It has been stated, apparently on the strength of a *Daily Telegraph* cable message, that O'Donovan Rossa before his death said that he had lost his hatred of the British Government and hoped the Irish would stand united in helping to fight Germany, the common enemy of civilization. Have you corroboration as to this being his later views and if so do you think publicity could be given to it?'(5) We do not know what reply, if any, he received to this. On the eve of the funeral Nathan informed Birrell that the demonstration would be a big one. The railways expected 14,000 passengers, and all the more troublesome elements of the population would be there. 'Colonel Moore will be in the procession!' he added. ' I have an uncomfortable feeling that the Nationalists are losing ground to the Sinn Féiners and that this demonstration is hastening the movement.'(6)

The O'Donovan Rossa funeral was in August. In September twelve hundred Volunteers marched openly with their arms through Dublin, and in October the Citizen Army under James Connolly led a sham attack on Dublin Castle. Taking part in the manoeuvre was the Countess Markievicz who had been telling the members of the Citizen Army to pawn their shirts and buy guns. Early that week the military proposed action to stop the collecting of money for arms, but Birrell ruled that the risk of failure was too great. It would not be possible either to

53

prevent greater sums being sent from America for the purchase of arms or for the payment of men who were making a living out of the movement. Additional vigilance over importations would be more effectual.(7)

In November, Lord Midleton urged that the Volunteers should be disarmed and not permitted to parade, but Birrell countered by saying as usual that the Sinn Féin organization and their drilling were not to be taken seriously. To take notice of speeches made by crackbrained priests and other enthusiasts would only halt the slow growth of loyalty in Ireland. He had some fear of the use of bombs, he said, but of no revolutionary trouble. They were handicapped by the clause inserted by the Unionist Lord Parmoor in D.O.R.A. in that they could only bring offenders before a jury. The Government, however, were watching closely, and from day to day, the actions of the Sinn Féiners, but they would do more harm than good by any open attempt to suppress them. This would probably result in shooting, and divide the country in the middle of the war. And he added : 'I laugh at the whole thing.'

But this pooh-poohing of the protestations of the Unionists had gone much too far. It was not at all justified by the facts of the case, as Nathan made clear to Birrel on 22 November. The general situation then was 'bad and fairly rapidly growing worse', he said. The Nationalist Party had lost control of the country and, with the avowed purpose of preparing to resist conscription, the extremists were everywhere organising and gaining strength. 'If conscription is introduced in Ireland', he added, 'it will result in the immobilization of a considerable British force as far as the war is concerned.' This had an immediate effect. Birrell passed the word of warning to Redmond. The Irish Volunteers month by month were steadily increasing, he told him. Wherever there was a plucky priest and two or three men with a little courage the movement was stamped out, but unluckily such priests and laymen were not always to be found.(8) Nathan too became more forthright. In early December he saw Lord Midleton and Mr Evelyn Cecil, representing the Unionists, and told them that Ireland was going down the hill. Sinn Féin was edging out Mr Redmond, their Volunteers were doing much mischief, and the young priests who supported them were very extreme. He described the difficult part Red-

54

mond had to play. He had been honestly Imperial in the war, but by going as far as he had done he had lost his position in the country. The whole position obviously required the most careful handling, but Nathan left Midleton with the impression that his hands were tied because the Chief Secretary had decided to do nothing.(9) Subsequently, Nathan gave Dillon an account of his interview with the Unionist leaders. He found Dillon now regarding the state of Ireland and the Sinn Féin movement as very serious, but 'he still advised me to keep my hands off the organizers'.(10)

It is likely that Midleton was at fault in taking away from the interview the impression that Nathan would have liked to do something other than what he was allowed to do by Birrell. The actual position was that Birrell and Nathan worked as a team and that as often as not it was Nathan who applied the brake or recommended that it should be applied. Within a few days of meeting the Unionists he was telling Birrell for instance, that it would be a mistake 'to go for' a certain paper, a course presumably proposed by the military. 'It is very little known,' he wrote, 'and the article has been unnoticed in Ireland. The seizure of the printer's plant would probably be followed by a demonstration of armed volunteers in Phoenix Park, violent speeches and all the other troublesome manifestations of ill-feeling which I am so anxious to avoid while the conscription question is still pending. And', he added—very strangely in view of the alarming accounts he had been so recently giving to all and sundry – 'already there seem to me to be indications that the Irish Volunteer movement has spent some of its novel force'.(11) He had been going easy on the papers for some time. He doubted whether the suppression of the *Spark* by itself would be commensurate with the disadvantage of advertising it,(12) and he was 'averse to stirring up mud by taking action on the "beastly" article in *Nationality* about the execution of Nurse Cavell'.(13)

Dillon continued to advise the Government to go carefully. They should keep their hands off the Volunteer organizers, he urged, and he painted lurid pictures of what might happen if conscription were attempted in Ireland. Nathan told him, however, that if the making of such an attempt depended on the failure of Lord Wimborne's efforts to get 10,000 men before the end of the month (November) it would be made. The appeals that had been lately issued left the farmers' sons unmoved and it was only by getting at them that any more recruiting on an appreciable scale was to be done in Ireland.

Nathan remained on easy terms with Dillon, saw him from time to time, corresponded with him, and occasionally sent him the Sinn Féin papers to read although he did not envy him the task of doing so.(*14*) But Dillon upset him now and then, and made him question his honesty of purpose or method. He contrasted him unfavourably with Redmond, when talking to the Irish Unionists. Over the handling of a land case at Greenanstown, Stamullen, Co. Meath, Dillon had committed himself to assisting the tenants, but had queered Nathan's pitch by violently abusing the landlord's agent in public just after Nathan had privately approached him, at Dillon's request. A thing became of very great moment in Dillon's view when he had intervened; it was a question of keeping up his influence by showing his power, and Nathan found that understandable. 'I certainly share his view', he said, 'that it is tremendously to the interests of Ireland and largely to those of the Empire also that the position of the Nationalist party should be strengthened, so I am anxious that the Greenanstown tenants should be helped.'(*15*) Some months later he returned to the same theme. The *Freeman* had been on the warpath and Nathan explained why. 'Redmond and Dillon feel they must work up some cries for the sake of their own position in Ireland. No one is more anxious to see that position improved than I am and I don't know that I really mind much their abusing the Government and me personally in their '*Freeman*' with this object in view, but it detracts from my respect for the men and for that I am sorry.'(*16*)

Recruiting being the dominant issue it was at this time, everything and everybody had to be subordinated to it, including the notoriously independent-minded George Bernard Shaw, whose efforts to be helpful usually went astray. 'I have made a strong appeal to the War Office to do away with the silly oaths and tests that stick in the throats of Irish recruits,' he wrote in a letter to the *Freeman's Journal*. To this Birrell replied privately: 'I have read your screed with much interest. It won't get a single recruit, unless you have made up your own mind to enlist. I certainly agree about *Oaths* but as for abolishing them you might as well ask me to abolish the XXXIX Articles or strike the *Nots* out of the X Commandments. Do use a little Common-sense.'(*16a*) He sent a play to the Abbey Theatre which, Nathan said, would be looked upon as too much a recruiting play by the Irish and as an anti-recruiting play by the English. Its title, *O'Flaherty, V.C.*, would give Birrell an idea of its nature. Shaw himself, in a preface he composed later, described his play as 'a recruiting poster in disguise', but whatever it was it could never have won recruits for the British Army. The hero of the piece had gone to the war pretending to his rebel mother that it was against the English he would be fighting. He pooh-poohed a suggestion that King and Country had anything to do with it. Never having had a piece of land of his own, country meant little to him, 'and as for the King, God help him', he said, 'my mother would have taken the skin off my back if I'd ever let on to have any other king than Parnell'. The credit for the deed of valour which won him the Victoria Cross was also due to his mother for she had taught him to be more afraid of running away than of fighting. That was all there was to it.

W. F. Bailey was an excitable man(*17*) and, as a trustee of the Theatre, he hurriedly sent the play to the Military Authorities for their views while Shaw wrote to Nathan asking that the treatment of the play might not be such as to give countenance to the German view that he was a supporter of theirs. While awaiting Birrell's reactions, Nathan, who had met Shaw at Sir Horace Plunkett's place outside Dublin, acknowledged his letter. He had read the play, he said, 'with excitement and interest' and would tell Shaw in a day or two what it seemed to him had best be done having regard to the public interest, that of the Theatre, and also to thwart the German claim. When he wrote again he told Shaw that he had consulted confidentially several persons in whose judgement he had confidence. They were definitely of the opinion that the production of the play at that time would result in demonstrations which could do no good either to the Abbey Theatre or to the cause that, at any rate, a large section of Irishmen had made their own. By such demonstrations the fine lesson of the play would be smothered while individual passages would be given a prominence Shaw did not intend for them. 'I think', he added, 'and so does General Friend that the production of the play should be postponed . . .' We have not got Shaw's reply but inside a week Nathan was able to tell Birrell that Bernard Shaw's play had quietly dropped out after he had received two very decent letters from the playwright to which he had replied. The reply merely indicated that Bailey was one of the people Nathan had consulted. He would be in London shortly and would then give Shaw the views they held in common. 'Possibly, even more than he does,' Nathan added, 'I should like to see the play produced here with certain elisions to avoid hurting excited susceptibilities. Possibly when I myself am in London in a week or two's time you would allow me to go and see you not only with regard to the play but also about the big subject of this country where much is dark to me that you could I believe illumine.'(*18*)

Nathan and Shaw duly met and quickly got on to 'the big subject'. 'I told him', Nathan recorded, 'something of the state of affairs with the Sinn Féiners in Ireland. I suggested the possibility of some counteracting literature to the stuff they circulated and the necessity for it to be on rather a high plane. He asked me to send him copies of leaflets issued by the Sinn Féiners and also by the Recruiting Department and he would see what he could do.' As soon as he returned to Dublin Nathan sent Shaw copies both of recruiting and anti-recruiting literature. In a covering letter (11 December 1915) he said : 'I have no doubt that the appeal to the Irish volunteers to fight for Ireland in Ireland has recently brought to the side of the single-minded Irish patriots – whom I respect while I believe them to be wrong in judgement and know them to be dangerous in effect – a number of persons who appreciate a patriotism which at the present time saves them from fighting at all. What is wanted is to destroy the public opinion which sanctions a man remaining neutral and to create a belief that the stirring up of hatreds at this time cannot but hinder the task of restitution and reconciliation on which the present prosperity of Ireland [depends] and the scheme for a reconstruction of its government on which England had seriously embarked. But this is ludicrously difficult.'

O'Flaherty V.C. was not the only play that aroused the interest of Dublin Castle at that time. In the middle of November

1915 *For the Land She Loved,* a piece in the tradition of the patriotic plays usually produced at the Queen's Theatre, was put on at the Abbey, and Nathan got his secretary to speak to Mr St John Ervine, the Theatre Manager, about it. The explanation given was that Mr P. J. Bourke who was the author, manager and chief actor in the production had not been able to get the Queen's, that it was not the sort of play the Abbey went in for, and that Mr Ervine would not have approved of giving the theatre to Mr Bourke had he known, which he did not, of the arrangement beforehand.(*19*)

Nathan made some use of the personal approach to counteract the Irish Volunteer movement. He spoke once more to Dr Denis J. Coffey, the President of University College, Dublin, on the strength presumably of the government's subsidy, about the propaganda that was being made within the College for the Volunteers and against enlistment in the Army. Coffey told him he would endeavour to check this in the first instance by getting hold of the students through the priests and others who inspected their lodgings. 'He did not think that the movement would have any dangerous results in the university as the present generation of students ... happened to be one very lethargic in their feelings and unlikely to be moved by persuasion.' Nathan asked Coffey about the two professors who took a leading part in the Volunteer movement. 'He (Coffey) referred as usual to Professor [Eoin] MacNeill as being full of chimeras and an unpractical man. Professor [Thomas] MacDonagh was the more dangerous of the two. He would try to make an opportunity of talking with them.' And as the interview ended, Nathan expressed some regret that circumstances had made it impossible for him to get into communication with any of the leaders of the 'present dangerous movement'.(*20*) One of the men he would have liked to have met, we imagine, was MacNeill who was influential in Gaelic League as well as Volunteer circles. The Gaelic League since July had become openly political, a fact that caused Dillon on two occasions to discuss with Nathan the possibility of a new non-political language organization. Douglas Hyde could form such a body, he said, but he feared that he would be too timid to do so.

As the year 1915 drew to an end the general war situation

was as bad as could be. The Germans had been victorious everywhere, and had inflicted appalling losses on the allies. The withdrawal from the Dardanelles was a particularly heavy blow to British prestige. Now it was inevitable that there would be some form of conscription, but the Coalition Cabinet was divided as to whether it should be applied to Ireland. On this depended, in the eyes of the Irish Executive and of the Irish Parliamentary leaders, whether Sinn Féin was to continue to be a force in the land.

Nathan continued to work like a galley slave without showing any ill effects but on Christmas Eve he entered in his diary 'Feeling rather seedy, the result of the war-time running down and the fifteen months of over-pressure.' Those who worked under him felt no better. He had appointed Joseph Brennan to be his Private Secretary with the departure to the Recruiting Office in Nassau Street of Kurten who later went to the war and was killed in 1918. Brennan told the present author that Nathan, 'a very human man', piled on the pressure at such a rate that he nearly killed those round him. This behaviour was largely unconscious and arose from the fact that he was so accessible. Brennan never knew a higher public servant that it was easier to approach. He saw everybody who asked to see him, on every conceivable subject, if only for a few minutes, and then dictated a note of the interview to his shorthand writer. At the end of a long trying day he would sit down and compose a detailed letter to Birrell which Brennan had to copy in long hand while the dispatch rider waited to take it to the mail-boat. Nathan, Brennan said, kept Birrell informed of everything that went on. Yet he found time to go visiting the poor of Dublin with James MacMahon of the Post Office who was an active member of the Society of St Vincent de Paul. This was prompted in part no doubt by an interest in discovering for himself how the poor lived; but his charity was also engaged, and he bespoke the patronage of Lady Wimborne for a Boys Club run by the past pupils of Clongowes College and for the St Vincent de Paul night shelter for homeless men.

Apart from Birrell's witty letters there was little in the way of light relief in Nathan's correspondence. However, Brennan, on a visit to his native Cork, wrote an account of the exercise of the Postal censorship in that part of Ireland that must have raised a smile on Nathan's face. The people of Cork city had been much disturbed by the sounds of hilarity proceeding from the Imperial Hotel and when they went to see what was causing it they found the military and a staff of lady censors engaged in reading the natives' letters out to each other while an audience in the street shared the fun.

CHAPTER EIGHT

'Things are fairly quiet here', Nathan told Birrell as the year 1916 opened. 'We still get spasmodic reports of new branches of Irish Volunteers formed, of organizers' visits, and one ruffian visiting another in Dublin, but I do not observe the acceleration of a triumphant movement and no conscription would mean its retardation.'(1) But the detective work of the Dublin police, the D.M.P., was of a poor quality.(2) By the middle of February 'nothing much had happened of late' though Nathan mentioned two things that had pleasantly surprised him. Dillon had agreed that the Castle was right in paying no attention to complaints from Monaghan which were attributable to a bad set of priests there; and a clever young man, who had been editing a paper that was openly antagonistic to the Government, had thrown up the job and joined a Training Corps.

General Friend took a much more pessimistic view of the situation and when he conferred with Birrell early in February following certain lawless proceedings in Dublin, Cork and other places he expressed the opinion that strong measures should be taken to assert lawful authority. The easiest way would be to proclaim the Irish Volunteers and forbid their meetings. He knew that this might be a matter for the Cabinet and that Birrell doubted the possibility of carrying a more repressive policy with the Government. The subject may never in fact have been discussed at Government level but the Prime Minister could be relied upon to support Birrell's line whatever it happened to be. Friend told his chief, General Lord French who was Commander of the Home Forces, of this conference, and on 14 February French saw Birrell who said he did not much fear these Volunteers, but would be glad to see them get a real good 'knock'. He thought Cork and Dublin the danger spots

62

but the danger to be apprehended was not so much a rising as secret outrages, dynamiting and so on.(*3*) He thought that troops marching about with bands would have a good effect. Birrell also said that the Royal Irish Constabulary were lethargic and not much good for detective purposes, an interesting comment on a force that was traditionally regarded as the eyes and ears of the Government in the areas outside Dublin.

The substance of what Birrell said to French was repeated to Friend who was asked to suggest the numbers of men likely to be required by him, and their location and composition, if it became necessary to back the police. Friend supplied the particulars, and in doing so supported Birrell's judgement by saying that he did not think any direct act of rebellion in force was likely. Nevertheless an addition of four Field Battalions would have a salutary effect and would counteract the anti-recruiting work of the Sinn Féiners.

Nathan's comment on these developments was that 'strong measures – or the appearance of them – are put on one side for the time being, I am sure rightly', although they might have to deal specially with Kerry.(*4*) And to regularize the position French told the Chief of the Imperial General Staff how things stood as a result of his conversation with Birrell, and he told Friend that he did not see that action could be taken so long as the Government did not think it urgent. Field troops were not available to send to Ireland except in a great emergency; the utmost that could be done at that time would be to send Reserve Brigades which could not, of course, be split up into detachments; or they might manage to send a Mounted Brigade. Friend thought he could manage to carry on as he was with certain arrangements to meet a sudden emergency, that he could not march troops about, as Birrell had suggested so that the public could see them, without upsetting training, but that a Mounted Brigade would be acceptable for such a purpose.

Nathan was in London in February and went to see Birrell who was ill, and was there again in March, indisposed himself and the recipient of kind enquiries from Dillon. When he got back to the Castle in the middle of the month he sent Dillon a note of thanks addressing him as 'My dear Dillon' and wondering whether their relations were not such as to justify dropping titles.(*5*) Dillon was doubting the wisdom of trying to get temporary Second Division Clerks in the Civil Service to enlist with the alternative of discharge(6) and was still averse to action against the seditious newspapers. The military had suggested smashing up the Gael Press which would have the effect of stopping 'three of the most violent but less circulated papers'. The objections to doing so were obvious – 'the unlikelihood of producing any but the most temporary effect on the others and the misrepresentations as to suppression of opinion that the action will give rise to more especially in America'. Also, the very violence of a particular article complained of seemed to make it ineffectual. On the other hand, to pass over the article would encourage the papers that were keeping within some bounds to exceed them, and might produce irritation in England 'when it was seen that this was done in opposition to military wishes'. The argument in favour of action won the day and Nathan told Birrell that 'on the whole, I am inclined, *pace* Dillon, to let the War Office do as it thinks fit in this matter'.(7) The 'coercionist' was now developing in Dillon as well as the 'Imperialist',(8) but this impression did not last. Within a few days the Gael printing press was seized and Birrell was told that 'at Liberty Hall (the Labour and Citizen Army headquarters) they are evidently fearing seizure of the *Workers' Republic,* but that is not yet'.

The Unionist pressure continued. On 20 January, Midleton saw Birrell and called his attention to speeches made by Father Michael O'Flanagan suggesting that Ireland should be an independent country in alliance with Germany, and to a circular from the Cork Irish Volunteers declaring that opposition to conscription must be backed by armed resistance. Birrell passed the buck; he suggested that Midleton should go over to Ireland and see General Friend. Midleton replied that he was quite willing to do this if the Government had some positive action in view, otherwise he would be wasting his time. Birrell then described the line the Irish Parliamentary Party were continuing to take, to which Midleton retorted that it was understandable that Redmond would not urge strong measures against those who were likely to prove a serious political embarrassment to him at the next election, but that did not relieve the Government of their responsibility. Midleton counselled Birrell to repeal the Parmoor clause, to take prompt measure to reassure the loyal element in Ireland so as to enable recruiting, which was being grievously affected, to be carried on. The discussion ended with Birrell stating his conviction that, despite what was taking place, there would be no armed rising, and he dwelt on the numerous reports he had which were not accessible to Midleton. The Unionist was not impressed. 'I told him frankly that I thought he was pursuing a dangerous course.'(9)

A month later (25 February 1916) when Nathan was in London Birrell sent Midleton a confidential letter suggesting that he should take up an invitation from Nathan for an interchange of ideas. 'He and I and the military authorities', Birrell wrote, 'are watching affairs and reports which reach us daily from all parts of Ireland very closely with a view to action when thought beneficial. I daresay I do not look at things quite from the same point of view which you would do were you in my place, though our objective would be the same. I want to promote, both by action and inaction, the growth of loyalty towards the Empire in the new Ireland which under the joint operation of the Land Acts and the Local Government Acts, chiefly Unionist measures, has sprung into being of late years. Loyalty in Ireland is a plant of slow growth and the soil is still uncongenial, but the plant grows though the old standing army of planters and waterers have all disappeared. Landlords, Grand Juries, Loyalist Magistrates have all gone, yet the plant grows, though slowly. I am not surprised when in Kerry and Cork and Galway and Clare I see signs of disloyalty and disaffection, whereas you seem annoyed and irritated and feel disposed to cry out for strong measures when headstrong priests and crack-brained people pass resolutions and make speeches which were they made and passed in England would bring down upon their promoters not the terrors of the law but the rage of the mob. Strong measures when effective are the best of all measures and the easiest, but if ineffective are no good but only harm. We cannot rely upon juries in Ireland, as the McCabe case in Dublin recently mournfully exhibited, but owing to Loreburn and Parmoor in your House we are woefully restricted. We have arrested and deported from place to place mischievous organisers, and I should be glad if you would talk to Nathan on this part of the case. To proclaim the Irish Volunteers as an illegal body and put them down by force wherever they appear would in my opinion be

65

a reckless and foolish act and would promote disloyalty to a prodigious extent. Huge exaggerations exist. In to-day's *Times* there is a letter from Mr Morgan O'Connell describing an interference to a recruiting meeting in Kilkenny. If you read the police report you would dismiss the whole affair from your mind. I am more alarmed at the possibility of bombs and isolated acts of violence than of concerted action, but see Nathan.'

Midleton, with Lord Barrymore, the President of the Irish Unionist Alliance, accordingly saw Nathan on 28 February. It was less than three months since they had met before; in the interval 'the movement' had developed much more seriously in Dublin, Nathan told them. He mentioned the names of those who were known to the Government as the chief conspirators and invited Midleton to read, as a specimen of what was being written, an article by Sheehy Skeffington in a recent number of the *Century*. Midleton left the meeting feeling so strongly that Nathan had not the necessary powers that he went up to the Phoenix Park to see the Lord Lieutenant. It is evident, however, that Nathan's concern for more power was limited to the problem of trial by jury. He was not quarrelling with the general policy of minimum action and maximum inaction that he was administering. On the contrary, he believed that this was the right policy and that his function was to prevent it from being upset. For instance, when Midleton next asked for an interview, Nathan jumped at the opportunity. It would enable him, he told Birrell, to keep Midleton quiet and this was something he thought he could do.(*10*)

When they met on this occasion, Midleton referred to the manifesto of the Volunteers which the *Daily Express* had published – an act which had caused Nathan to remonstrate with the editor – and this began an overall discussion on drilling and bombs, the development of the 'movement' in Cork, publications by the Dublin newspapers, and the necessity of armed action, arrests and further deportations. Nathan had nothing really new to say in his reply. The Government were still relying on the advice given them by Redmond and Dillon, and Midleton could only protest once more against their shirking of responsibility, especially as Sir Matthew was alive to the fact that he was dealing with desperate men.(*11*) Midleton, a few days later, again went to see the Lord Lieutenant who was a kindred spirit. He found him much more concerned about the situation than he had been six weeks earlier and most anxious to deal with some of the ringleaders. But Midleton gathered that he was unable to move further owing to the general attitude of the Government which it was impossible to disturb.

CHAPTER NINE

Wimborne had been asserting himself as best he could. He was no longer content with an occasional meeting with Birrell or Nathan, or with Friend in his capacity as Competent Military Authority; he was inquisitive about all their affairs and wanted to be involved in them. He had begun his viceroyalty by making a point of seeing members of the Nationalist Party in the Lobby of the House of Commons, and of lunching with some of them. Redmond told him of his intention of writing his name in the Viceregal Book, a matter the Lord Lieutenant considered significant enough to mention to Nathan,(1) who agreed that it would indeed be an achievement to get politicians of different sides to meet at a place where there were no politics.(2) Wimborne's recruiting activities had brought him more into the picture, but he pointed out to Nathan the absurdity of the Lord Lieutenant having to rely on the press for his knowledge with regard to current administrative matters – and it was symptomatic of the situation that it was to Nathan he should have spoken – and the practical inconvenience which resulted from being kept in ignorance on subjects which were constantly referred to by persons he met. Nathan gave him a perfectly frank but polite statement of the superior position of the Chief Secretary deriving from past history, as well as from his Cabinet rank; however, as Wimborne was so insistent, he thought it wiser to lift the veil gradually for him. The result of this was that Nathan had a regular and persistent correspondent on his hands. He first sent him, with explanatory notes, the monthly recruiting and state of the country returns with particulars of prosecutions, but then found he had to answer questions about them. In this way, it emerged that in the month to the middle of February 1916, there had been 2,189 recruits, which was not a very satisfactory figure; but the stream continued to trickle. The prosecutions that month disclosed no serious state of affairs, however; there were only seventeen in all and nine of these arose out of the supply of drink. As to 'crimes' of a political character, there were three of persons wearing uniform without authority; a fine had been imposed for selling ammunition, and a case was still pending of a man who had been found making notes with regard to a patrol boat. A Claude Chavasse had achieved some notoriety by refusing to answer reasonable questions to the best of his ability; although an Englishman he had insisted on answering the questions in Irish.

But Wimborne wanted to get even closer to the real issues. In the middle of March he induced Nathan to send him up the daily D.M.P. reports, and on these, as on everything else he got, the Viceroy commented, sometimes rather trenchantly. He got Nathan to tell Friend in his capacity as Competent Military Authority that the Executive – in which he doubtless now began to include himself – should have had previous cognisance of a so-called search for arms in Cork which had been made for the purpose of providing the Crown Solicitor with information against the signatories of an appeal for funds for the Volunteers.(3) He took a particular interest and pleasure in the policy of deportation. The Government had hitherto been handicapped by the limitations of the law. Internment in Ireland required proof of actual association with the German enemy which could not be furnished and when Orders were made deporting individuals they could not be implemented. The Regulations under the Defence of the Realm Act had, therefore, to be strengthened and it was in this month of March, 1916, that Wimborne was assured that the Competent Military Authority was now in a position to clear out of Ireland those individuals who had made themselves particularly obnoxious as Volunteer organizers. There were four of these 'Banishees', as Birrell called them : Ernest Blythe, William Mellowes, Alfred Monaghan and A. W. Cotton – and some other organizers on whom an eye was being kept, T. J. McSweeney, J. J. O'Connell, Peter O'Hourihane, John O'Hurley, Denis McCullough and Herbert M. Pim.

Nathan confessed to feeling a little bit worried on 24 March; he did not say why, but a week before, on St Patrick's Day, the Irish Volunteers had for the first time taken what a journalist described as 'aggressive action in daylight' in the centre of

Dublin, the whole force assembling in College Green where they gave a display of military manoeuvres and then marched past their President, Eoin MacNeill. These operations lasted two hours during which traffic was peremptorily suspended by the Volunteers most of whom carried rifles and bayonets.(4) That day at a Castle Conference, the question of breaking up armed manoeuvres was discussed and Nathan recorded 'Chief Commissioner handed list of meetings and pointed out difficulties. If ordered to disperse would probably do so'. This does not seem to have been tried.(5) And four days earlier (20 March) there had been disturbances in Tullamore, culminating in a shooting affray in a Sinn Féin Hall, in the course of which several policemen were injured before arrests were made. The R.I.C. reports summarised by French for the Adjutant General indicated that 'certain parts of Ireland were in a very disturbed state and that insurrection had been openly suggested in the public press'. French wondered had Birrell changed the opinion he had expressed a short time previously that he did not anticipate open insurrection. He drew attention to the seriousness of even a small rising in Ireland and suggested that a Proclamation should at once be issued restoring the right of trial by court-martial in specified cases. He had little hope that the persons arrested for the Tullamore business would be convicted if tried by jury. Alternatively he recommended changing the venue to England.

A conference was held in London on 23 March between French and 'the Irish Government Authorities' and the suggestion was there made and conveyed to the War Office that the garrisons in Ireland should be increased and that one or more Reserve Infantry Brigades from England should be permanently stationed in Ireland. French had no objection to this from a Home Defence point of view but the adoption of the proposal would delay training, possibly complicate draft-finding and entail other disadvantages. No action was taken about the substitution of court-martial for trial by jury. Indeed it was said that the Prime Minister had scotched such a proposal somewhat earlier, but Asquith had no recollection of having done so when the matter was later brought to his notice. On 25 March the Government moved against two of the 'Banishees'. Blythe and Mellowes were arrested and conveyed to the place of detention at Arbour Hill to await removal to the area in England where they might elect to reside.(6) Blythe declined to elect a residence and was seen into the train at Abingdon on his way to Wood-stock in Oxfordshire where he was ordered to remain. Mellowes elected to reside at Leck in Staffordshire, and 'when well out to sea' was supplied with a ticket to go there. The police at Liver-pool and Holyhead had been directed to detain in the event of any attempt being made to return and the local police were instructed to communicate with Dublin if the deportees left their areas. If they got back to Ireland their presence would not matter there; but if they started their old games they would be returned to England and tried there for disobedience of the Competent Military Authority's order.

At the meeting on 17 March 1916, at which these decisions were taken, it was also decided that Alfred Monaghan was to be ordered out of Ireland, the papers regarding A. W. Cotton were to be studied by General Friend, the question of clearing Kerry was to be looked at again, and the Attorney General was to consider whether action could be taken against T. J. Clarke on the basis of a former sentence, this because of some American correspondence that had come under notice.(7)

The Government's action disturbed Dillon. He had some very disquieting news from the country, he told Nathan on 26 March, and was anxious to communicate it and to discuss it but 'I really *can't* go to the Castle', he said, and as at the Congested Districts Board or in any other public office they would be far more under observation, he had no alternative but to ask Nathan to come to see him in North Great George's Street, on his way to or from the office. Nathan did and gave him some reports to read on the state of the country but, having read them, Dillon was critical and wondered whether the situation had been improved by the action taken against the organizers and the newspapers. 'To me', he said, 'it appears that the tension has been seriously increased' (31 March 1916).

A number of anti-deportation meetings were held; but the passion for them speedily spent its force.(8) 'The one (in Dublin) on Thursday', Nathan told Birrell (7 April 1916), 'attracted the rowdy element in the town and this seems a little to have alarmed the leaders.' Revolver shots were fired in Grafton Street and opposite the Provost's House in Trinity College, and one of these pierced a pocket in the overcoat of a police inspector;

71

but the only charge made was against a young man for being a member of a disorderly crowd and breaking a lamp in a motor car. 'I think we will watch the effect of these (deportation) measures before starting new ones of the same nature. I hope no more will be necessary for the present. I shall be disappointed if while attempts are being made to raise troops in Ireland English troops are demobilized to keep Ireland in order. . . . Nothing of special interest is taking place at the moment. . . .'(9)

Meanwhile, the Adjutant General was considering the report of French's conference of 23 March. He wrote privately to Friend, expressing certain 'opinions' which we have not got, and said that he presumed that if Friend concurred in the desirability of sending Reserve Infantry Brigades to Ireland he would make an official application to that effect. Friend replied (7 April) : 'in the event of having to take serious action in support of the Royal Irish Constabulary against the disloyal organizations, I should be glad to have one or two additional brigades from England, and I would then, if all went well, ask for such troops to be left here for some months, to aid recruiting as fast as possible; but at the present moment these anxieties are not quite so great as they were. Under these circumstances, and in view of the opinions you send me I do not propose to put forward an official application for additional troops to be sent for recruiting purposes.' A copy of this letter of Friend's was sent by the Adjutant General's office to French on 12 April with an intimation that no further action was deemed necessary at present. It was possible to say this on the strength more particularly of a reply that the Adjutant General had just received from Nathan.

He had told Nathan privately that French had represented officially that certain parts of Ireland were in a very disturbed state, that insurrection had been suggested in the press, that he thought Birrell might have changed his views as to the probability of a Rising and that he recommended that a Proclamation should be issued under Article 58 of the Defence of the Realm Act. What did he think of this in view of French's proposals for strengthening the Irish Garrisons and so forth. Nathan replied without hesitation (10 April). Regarding a rising in Ireland he was very positive. 'Though the Irish Volunteer element has been active of late,' he said, 'especially in Dublin, *I do not believe that its leaders mean insurrection or that the Volun-*

72

teers have sufficient arms if the leaders do mean it. (The Prime Minister underscored the second half of that sentence as we have done when he read it some weeks later.) The bulk of the people are not disaffected and even in such an uncompromising county as Clare we obtained within the last few days the conviction of an Irish Volunteer under the regulations, from the local bench.

'I think it is unfortunate as far as Ireland is concerned that the amended Act giving option of trial by jury to British subjects was passed, but much more trouble than I anticipate in the near future should, I think, precede any proclamation which would result in the suspension of its operation in Ireland alone.'

The very day Nathan delivered this opinion the Director of Military Intelligence in London received an appraisal of the situation also from Major Price, the Intelligence Officer attached to the Irish Command. Price detailed the number of Irish Volunteers in the various counties and, while stating that the population in general was loyal, he remarked that the Sinn Féin Volunteers were practising drill, rifle shooting, night attacks and holding officer training schools. They had been collecting arms, and had considerable funds at their disposal. They were stealing rifles and explosives, and hand grenades made by them had recently been seized by the police at Leixlip near Dublin. Five hundred bayonets had been seized in the previous week and on 9 April a number of guns, revolvers and bayonets had been taken while being conveyed from Dublin to Wexford by Sinn Féiners. There was undoubted proof that Sinn Féin Irish Volunteers were working up for rebellion and revolution, if ever they got a good opportunity. Price said he had read this report to General Friend who fully concurred in it. A copy of the report was handed to a member of French's staff on 11 April, and was considered both by French and by the War Office. It did not disclose anything particularly new, French thought, beyond giving them for the first time some definite estimate of the strength and armament of the Sinn Féin party. Nor did it change the military position which still depended on Birrell's previously expressed opinion, which, so far as French knew, remained unaltered.

There was a 'bad incident', on Sunday 9 April, during another big Irish Volunteer parade in Dublin. A tram car was held up

73

by an unidentified volunteer pointing a revolver at the driver. And on the same day the police, at Nathan's direction, captured, as Major Price had reported to the Director of Military Intelligence, a motor car that had loaded up with arms at Father Matthew Park and was on its way to the Volunteers at Ferns, Co. Wexford. But these things did not unduly worry Nathan apparently and on 13 April he told Birrell that things were going better for the moment. 'The deportations certainly did good in the country, and the small capture of arms and the prompt punishment of the men who were carrying them will be good for Dublin.' And he added: 'We are at last getting some information as to what is going on here – for the first time since I have been in the place.'(10) Wimborne, too, thought they had reason to be satisfied with the result of their greater anti-Sinn Féin activities. If the deportations already effected proved a success, more might follow. He thought that 'Clarke, Connolly and others whom I don't remember might... themselves be destined for a similar excursion'.(11)

The reports the Castle was at last getting seem to have come from men whom they had placed within the ranks of the Volunteers; they were wholly in the nature of hearsay, however, and Friend when he read the earlier ones 'attributed no great importance' to them.(12) One of these reports early in March said that 'a notification had been received from Germany that it was their intention to strike a final blow... and requested the Irish Volunteers to be ready to render their promised assistance....' It was stated that this information was only in the possession of prominent pro-German members and of the organizers. A Dublin informer reported on 16 March that the young men of the Irish Volunteers were very anxious to start business at once and they were being backed up strongly by Connolly and the Citizen Army but that the heads of the Irish Volunteers were against a Rising at present. Thomas MacDonagh (one of the principal Volunteer officers) was stated to have said that it would be sheer madness to attempt such a thing if the help promised by Monteith, who was in Germany, was not forthcoming. From the same source it was reported on 27 March that MacDonagh, addressing a meeting of Volunteers five days before, had told them, with reference to the Tullamore affray which had ended in the R.I.C. disarming some volunteers, that had instructions been carried out not one policeman would have crossed the door alive. A general mobilization had been called for 2 April. Another Dublin informer, reporting on the same day, said that there was, at present, no fear of a rising by the Volunteers. Standing alone they were not prepared for any prolonged encounter with the forces of the Crown and the majority of them were practically untrained. On 31 March the Dublin informer who had given warning of the mobilization of the Volunteers on 2 April for which everybody was alerted said that this had been cancelled.

In the order of opinion as distinct from 'information' Nathan had the benefit of Mrs Green's views. She had had an opportunity of seeing a few people, priests and others, closely concerned in the Irish Volunteers, and had several frank conversations. 'It would have given you a surprise to hear them,' she told him on 14 April. 'What I have heard confirms my view that whatever underground work there may be is unknown, not only to the chiefs, but to the general body of confidential organizers who are straight, honest young men. There is not the same soil for evil counsels to grow in as there was thirty years ago.' She was very critical of Redmond, and admired the Volunteers. Redmond was mad to let all this good material slip out of his hands. 'When', she asked, 'will there be an old man with a heart young enough to lead the young with his experience? With all the bungling and foolish leadership, perhaps the Volunteers are a force for order rather than disorder.'(*13*)

While keeping up the regular supply of reports to the Chief Secretary, Nathan occasionally picked out an optimistic bit for comment. 'Some rather bad Orange proceedings at Portadown', which sent him looking for Devlin in a hurry, had had no sequel. The incident at Tullamore had ended satisfactorily with a display of local feeling against the Sinn Féin people. The recruiting figures from Dublin – about 450 – were better than the previous month and than Belfast, and the grand total for the country as a whole came to about 1,700 (*14*) But there were other and more unwelcome things. What was Tennant up to sending men to the Recruiting Department who were worse than useless? 'Sheehan M.P. drinks as well as being distasteful to the Parliamentary party and of Sir Francis Vane ghastly tales are told. Both were forced on Friend by Tennant and the appointment of the second was made a personal matter by Lord French. The Recruiting Department fear both to keep him in the office or to send him to the country lest he should do serious harm to their work. The matter is a complete mystery to us here. Can you find out from Tennant why it was necessary to employ these men?'(*15*) Later he sought Birrell's permission to write to Tennant 'about those two ruffians'. A Post Office official had come home on leave: was he just dodging military service or plotting with his brother-in-law Cornelius Collins, who was constantly in the company of pro-German suspects.(*16*) A Post Office doctor, Edward Dundon, had been mischievous. He was being watched and if, despite action already taken against him, he had further connection with the Irish Volunteers, Norway would be authorized to dispense with his services.(*17*) The problem of sedition in print was unending: the suppressed papers were replaced by others; the Irish papers produced in America added fuel to the fire. *The Gaelic-American* and *The Irish World* were now stopped in London on their way to Ireland but arrangements had to be made to ensure that some of the seized copies were made available to Redmond, Dillon, Devlin and the *Freeman's Journal* for their particular purposes. And Needham, the Recruiting Officer, drew attention to the Sinn Féin tendencies of *The Irish Independent*. This was surely the last straw. The anti-recruiting campaign was particularly intensive, and Nathan was not allowed to overlook it. James C. Percy, an honorary recruiting officer for the Royal Navy, sent him a copy of Connolly's newspaper, *The Workers' Republic,* which contained what he described as a scandalous attack on Father Doherty, a speaker at some of their meetings. The paper said in effect—'His Holiness the Pope does not ask us to recruit; His Grace Archbishop Walsh does not ask us to recruit, and here is this whippersnapper of a priest from Marlboro' Street asking Ireland to lay down their lives for this rotten Empire'.(*18*)

The police were now posted at the front and back of 44 Parnell Square, Dublin, where the National Volunteers had their arms stored. The Commissioner of the D.M.P. was informed that the Sinn Féiners, who apparently had plenty of money, were still trying to purchase arms from individual National Volunteers and were ready to steal them if they could not get them by other means. The National Volunteer leaders were again asked

76

to watch this, but the truth of the matter was that the disintegration of the National Volunteers was far advanced. There were other signs too that the Nationalist Party were being intimidated by the active and noisy minority, and required police protection for their public meetings. Police action was, however, not always discriminating enough. Their activity in South Derry was calculated, Dillon believed, to promote the Sinn Féiners' propaganda. 'Surely the police ought to be instructed to stop these enquiries,' he said (1 April 1916).

Dillon was trying to get other things stopped too, as Nathan told Birrell. 'I have stopped their (the military) dealing with Irishmen who have come from England to avoid enlistment until I can put all the facts of the case before you and advise what should be done. They number some twelve or thirteen hundred and Dillon is a bit fussed over them. He is troubled also over temporary (unassigned) 2nd Division Clerks here being given the option of enlistment or no re-employment at the end of their present job; over a land squabble on a petty estate at Kiltimagh and over one or two other matters. I will go to him one day this week and clear up things with him'.(*19*) Nathan continued to be concerned about appointments that might be obnoxious to the Nationalists. James Campbell, a Unionist K.C., had been made Attorney General in spite of the emphatic protest of the Irish Party. It was, Dillon said, a very great outrage, and might lead to very serious and deplorable consequences.(*20*) Nathan did not like the appointment even on personal grounds for he had formed the impression of rather a bullying personality. He saw the danger also of the appointment of Shannon following on that of Campbell. 'The appointment of Robertson (which I should like to see because he is the man who gets the convictions for us) would be no better from the Nationalist point of view especially as it would involve the direct passing over of Lynch who is Robertson's senior in the office. The Catholic who has received most backing is Sir John O'Connell—a decent little man—very little—who has done a good deal of public work. Do you know anything of him?'(*21*) But these matters, important though they were, were overshadowed by the rapid growth of an atmosphere of crisis which Mr Justice Kenny described at the opening of the Green Street Commission (11 April 1916). It was a time of grave and unexampled tension, he said, in which the very existence of the United Kingdom was involved, and in which every man was expected to do his utmost according to his ability and opportunity. Some could join the Forces, others could help with munitions, a large section could devote their energies to the care of the wounded—but it was difficult for any of these things to be a complete success in the face of a propaganda of an openly seditious character and one which seemed to set all authority at defiance. And he elaborated on the various forms of activity which tended to paralyze the recruiting movement, and to have the most mischievous influence on certain classes of people.(22)

The crisis being produced by Sinn Féin was not the only one. As Easter drew near, a crisis within the Cabinet blew up over conscription and there was a real danger of a change of Government. Nathan did not welcome the prospect; he could not, he said, accept it with the same stoicism as Birrell did. 'But it will be all right if it be only a shuffling of the cards and you fall in the same hand as before.'(23) There would be a break for holidays at Easter, and Nathan was looking forward to it. He had arranged that his sister-in-law, Estelle, would come over with her family and risk the German submarines reported to have been seen in the Irish sea. And 'I look forward to seeing you at Easter', he told Birrell. "Will you be going to the Viceregal Lodge or can I put you up : I can do so but less confidently as the house will be full of children.'(24)

CHAPTER TEN

On 17 April, Monday of Holy Week, Friend handed Nathan a letter he had received from Brigadier General W. F. H. Stafford, who commanded the Queenstown defences which included eight southern counties and extended from the north of Co. Clare to Arklow. It told of a contemplated landing of arms and ammunition on the south-west coast and a rising fixed for the following Saturday, Easter Eve. Nathan showed the letter to Neville Chamberlain, the Inspector General of the R.I.C., and although they were both 'doubtful whether there was any foundation for the rumour', they thought it well to put the County Inspectors in the southern and south-western counties on their guard. Nathan also told Edgeworth-Johnstone, the Chief Commissioner of the Dublin Metropolitan police, so that a watch might be kept on the 'turbulent suspects' in Dublin.(1) They may also have mentioned the matter to their informers; at any rate one of them reported on Wednesday, the 19th, that there was at that time no knowledge of any immediate importation of arms into Ireland.

On the same afternoon, Alderman Tom Kelly read to the Dublin Corporation a document which the censor had stopped *New Ireland* from publishing. This was described as a decipher of a paper on the official files of the Castle, giving details of an order that General Friend had signed for large-scale raids on buildings in the city, as part of a plan for disarming the Volunteers. The Government, it was alleged by Patrick J. Little, the editor of *New Ireland,* had embarked on this course with the intention of provoking armed resistance and deliberately causing bloodshed. It was officially denied that any such document existed or ever existed; and some people saw through it immediately. Amongst the places specified for attention in the alleged order was the residence of the Catholic Archbishop of Dublin,

79

and, as a provincial paper suggested, no sane man in the country would regard a document with such a proviso as other than a figment. 'British Government in Ireland has done many assinine things,' the paper continued, 'but it is not, even in the face of a silly Sinn Féin scare, so bereft of sanity as to dream of interning the Reverend Metropolitan of the See of St Lawrence O'Toole, and when in Dublin a Sinn Féin Alderman tries to create a counter scare by asserting that it does, he is making a veritable fool of himself.'(2) Five months later Nathan studied the evidence, including the 'leaderettes' in *New Ireland* and came to the conclusion that many of the Volunteers were not in the councils of the leaders and were being worked upon by those holding out the possibility of disarmament.(3) However, the document was widely accepted and Professor Thomas MacDonagh, an Irish Volunteer Commandant, insisted that it was genuine, and had been put into their hands by friends of theirs in the Castle. This was reported by an informer who said that MacDonagh that Spy Wednesday night also told his men : 'We are not going out on Friday (Good Friday), but we are going on Sunday . . . Boys, some of us may never come back.' A time had been fixed for a general march out on Sunday, and arrangements made for safeguarding Volunteers in Government employment from being observed by the police.

That same night about nine o'clock while Nathan was dining with the Stopfords to meet Douglas Hyde, Edgeworth-Johnstone got information that there was to be a general mobilization of the Volunteers to be followed by an attack on Dublin Castle, apparently that night. 'Needless to say,' he told Nathan the next day, 'I did not believe the latter statement. However, as the Sinn Féiners began to assemble with arms (at various points) and the Transport Workers people at Liberty Hall I thought it wise to take no chance.' So he made dispositions and kept his men standing by until 11.15 when the Volunteers and the others dispersed. The same day, Dillon found Dublin full of the most disquieting rumours and told Redmond he was sure the Clann na Gael men were planning some devilish business.(4) He inquired later of Nathan whether he had any trustworthy information, and hoped the rumours were without foundation.

Holy Thursday (20 April) and most of Good Friday (21 April) passed quietly in the Castle although the D.M.P. reported the usual meetings of suspects; but on Good Friday night the Constabulary Office sent Nathan up a message which had come in from the County Inspector of Tralee to the effect that that morning a patrol from Ardfert, which is four or five miles from Tralee, had captured a boat, 1,000 rounds of ammunition, three Mauser pistols, and maps and papers, all German. They had arrested one prisoner and two had escaped. They were believed to have come from a Dutch vessel.

On 22 April (Easter Saturday) Nathan, in a letter to Birrell, described what had happened since 19 April. 'Today,' he went on, 'after receiving various incorrect reports, I have learned that a vessel, disguised as Norwegian, was stopped off the coast of Kerry and was being brought into Queenstown when it hoisted German colours and sank, being scuttled by the crew about a mile south of the lightship at Daunt's Rock at the entrance to the harbour. Nineteen German sailors and three officers were taken off it and are now in custody on the flagship.' This was the *Aud*, carrying arms for a rising. The man captured in Kerry the previous day was arriving at Kingsbridge at 5.30 that evening and would be sent with the maps and papers taken with him to England that night. 'A telegram from the County Inspector received this morning said that it is believed he is Sir Roger Casement. I shall probably know whether he is or is not that lunatic traitor before I send off this.' It was Casement, although Nathan first reported to Birrell that it was not. Other telegrams from the County Inspector at Tralee that day had told how a Limerick motor believed to belong to Sinn Féiners drove into the sea at Ballykissane Pier, Killorglin, the previous night, all the occupants being drowned except the driver; and that Austin Stack (formerly of the Labour Exchange Department of the Board of Trade) and Cornelius Collins of the Dublin Post Office, two of the Civil Servants that Nathan had earlier been concerned with, had been arrested at Tralee on a charge of conspiracy to land arms; they were being sent to Dublin. Nathan had asked Price, the Intelligence Officer, to tell the papers not to publish any information about these incidents unless the Admiralty made a communiqué.

He also told Birrell that the Irish Volunteers were to have a 'mobilization' and march out from Dublin on the following day (Easter Sunday) but, he added, 'I see no indications of a "rising" '. Nevertheless, he was very much inclined, he said, to 'go for' the two places in Dublin – Kimmage and Fr Matthew Park – where they believed the Sinn Féiners were manufacturing and storing arms and ammunition, but they were first trying to obtain a little more definite information with regard to them. Nathan asked Birrell when he was likely to be over in Dublin. There were two matters in particular he wanted to talk about. The Crown Solicitorship remained to be settled and the decision would create heartburning; and there were those Military Service Act cases. Dillon was very indignant that any action, even interrogating men returned from England, should be taken and seemed generally in a bad humour. So Nathan would like to see Birrell and hoped he now took a less despondent view of affairs than he did the previous week. Of himself, he said that he was fit 'and not knowing much of what is going on, am fairly cheerful'.(5) He had the trouble within the Cabinet in mind, but his words might have applied equally to the situation that was boiling up in the heart of Dublin. Birrell had intended to cross to Ireland that Easter Saturday but earlier in the week his secretary, A. P. Magill, a Dublin man, told Nathan that until the Cabinet crisis which was threatening to destroy the government developed one way or the other it was hard to make plans. Not being affected by the crisis himself, Magill hoped to come home for the Easter; but he did not like the way things were shaping in London and his chief, 'a cheerful pessimist', was having a depressing effect on those around him. However, on the 20th (Holy Thursday) Birrell returned from a Cabinet meeting and told Power, who was relieving Magill, that he thought the government would now survive. Power passed this tit-bit on to Nathan but said that Birrell had decided to stay at home for Easter.

Nathan saw Wimborne on Easter Saturday and he found him convinced that the happenings in Kerry had revolutionized the situation. He agreed with Nathan that the Sinn Féin Party would have been much dismayed by those events, that the menace of a rising could be considered at an end, that it had been probably contingent on the successful landing of arms and that, therefore, the prospect of future tranquillity was improved. The military had feared that when Casement was being brought up from Kerry an attempt at rescuing him would be made; but he had reached Dublin at five-thirty on Easter Saturday morning without apparently anybody knowing about his arrival, and he was on the boat for England before eight o'clock. The military shared the Government view that Casement was the key man in the whole business and, when next day, Easter Sunday, they read that the mobilization of the Volunteers fixed for that day was cancelled, they assumed it was because his mission had failed.

There remained the question of taking action against the Sinn Féiners, now that a definite connection between them and the King's enemies had been established, and Wimborne urged that no time should be lost in arresting and interning the Dublin leaders. But Nathan had taken no action in that regard at the close of Easter Saturday. He was arranging, however, to help the police by having some members of a loyal body known as the Irish Volunteer Training Corps in uniform wearing G.R. armlets sworn in as Special Constables for duty on certain public buildings, including the General Post Office, the Telephone Exchange and Arbour Hill Barracks. They would be provided with whistles and could provide themselves with sticks.(6)

At six o'clock on Easter Sunday morning (23 April) a message from Limerick told Nathan that Bailey, one of the men who had landed with Casement, had been captured at Tralee; the other, Monteith, another former Government employee on Nathan's list, was still missing. Bailey had made a full statement. He belonged to the Royal Irish Rifles and to the German Irish Brigade, and had come to Ireland in a submarine under the name of Beverley. He implicated Stack and Collins and stated that arms and ammunition were to be landed from a ship on Easter Saturday night or Easter Sunday and that there was to be a general rising on Easter Sunday. The *Sunday Independent*, however, on that morning carried a notice from Eoin MacNeill, the head of the Irish Volunteers, countermanding the parades and manoeuvres arranged for that day which confirmed the authorities in their conviction that the Rising was off.

But was it? Nathan was in his office in Dublin Castle by nine-thirty and an hour later when he called on the Lord Lieutenant he had the news for him that the Sinn Féiners had forcibly seized 250 pounds of gelignite from a quarry at Tallaght and taken it to Liberty Hall. The police had followed them there and were keeping the precincts under close observation. Nathan proposed to raid the Hall and the two other minor arsenals at Larkfield, Kimmage and Fr Matthew Park that night but Wimborne did not think this went far enough. He pressed Nathan to put his hands on the ringleaders, 'who, having countermanded their Easter Day Parade, are probably sitting in conclave conspiring against us'. He also suggested that the Castle guard should be strengthened but Nathan demurred. He gave no reason and Wimborne did not ask for one. It was now getting on to eleven o'clock, and Wimborne had formed the extraordinary idea, which he may have thought Nathan shared, that it was already too late for the Rising to take place that day. When he was asked subsequently if he meant that a rebellion should begin immediately after breakfast, he replied that it should not be put off until the afternoon as a rule! Nathan still hesitated about the arrests but he finally gave a qualified consent and later sent the Chief Secretary a cypher telegram which, however, did not reach Birrell until the next day (Easter Monday). This told of Bailey's arrest and continued: 'In view of definite association of Irish Volunteers with enemy now established I agreed with Lord Lieutenant that leaders should be arrested and interned in England. Can this be proceeded with subject to concurrence of the Law Officers, Military Authorities and Home Office?'

Wimborne wrote simultaneously to Birrell repeating his arguments. 'The evidence is now sufficient for any measure we think desirable. . . . The whole lot of them could be arraigned for associating with the King's enemies and there is our internment policy safely in port. I am afraid if you stir up the hornets' nest and leave the hornets that we may have serious trouble. . . . The capture of Casement was a stroke of luck, and reflected credit on the police and the executive. I hope there will be no nonsense about clemency. He must be made an example of. He expects nothing else, I understand. These fellows have enjoyed too much immunity already.' After all, their intention had been nothing else than to create a diversion in favour of the enemy and detain three or four divisions in Ireland to deal with it at a critical time in the war. 'I want to implicate as many of the Sinn Féiners as I can with the landing – the invasion, in fact. It has changed everything, and justifies our altering our attitude. A public trial, if there are not bad (?) difficulties in the way, would bring it

84

home best. . . . We shall never get a better opportunity. If you agree, do write and ginger Nathan. I have never made much of their movements or have been or am now an alarmist, but if you don't take your chances they do not recur.'

Birrell sent a reply that day (Easter Sunday) to Nathan's letter of the 22nd. At last something had happened, he said, and he hoped that the identification of Casement was true. He summarized 'the haul' – all of which, particularly if Roger Casement was the prisoner, was most encouraging.

'But who', he went on, 'can account for such a proceeding as the Vessel's – had the crew any grounds for a belief in a *rising*? It may be that the *Lunatic* being *disgraced in Germany* (as reported) was bound to make . . . this ridiculous effort. We seem to have been well served in the whole matter.

'The March of the *Irish Volunteers* will not be conducted in high spirits.

'If we can lay hands on stored arms and ammunition it would be good – so far our information has not been trustworthy.

'Redmond and Dillon are very much out of humour just now – it may be that Redmond will take the opportunity of this "Cabinet crisis" to recover some portion of his loss of authority by an outburst of *rhetoric*. I think he is sorry the Coalition is saved – if it be saved. He has cut off his *daily* connection with me and is lobbying on his own account. The Carsonic frontal attack will be (I suppose) withdrawn but there may be *side attacks* by Labour and Radicals . . . I think you may rely upon my being in Dublin by the end of this week – whatever happens I must come.'

He did come by the end of that week but in circumstances that showed that his optimism had been entirely misplaced.

Having sent off his telegram, Nathan returned to the Under-Secretary's Lodge and rejoined his sister-in-law, Estelle, who with her children and Mrs Stopford Green's niece, Dorothy, had settled in for the Easter holiday. Estelle and he had a luncheon appointment with Sir Horace Plunkett so he can't have delayed long at the Lodge before setting out on the journey to Kilteragh which lay out at Foxrock on the other side of the city. Lord and Lady Fingal were there, and the party were naturally excited by Nathan's account of the happenings of recent days. He assured them that all immediate danger had been averted with

Casement's arrest and the cancelling of the Volunteer parade. They could go to Fairyhouse Races on the morrow as had been planned, and Lady Fingal could take Mrs Nathan to see the show at the Abbey.(7)

Before six o'clock Nathan collected two staff officers, Colonel Cowan and Major Owen Lewis, in the absence of General Friend who had gone to England, and took them up to the Viceregal. On the way he told them about the gelignite and the proposed raid on Liberty Hall. He felt sure there would be considerable fighting. The raid would stir the large numbers of Volunteers who had collected for the much-advertised and now abandoned Easter demonstration and probably lead to trouble in other parts of Dublin as well. The result of this preliminary conversation was to raise some difficulties in the minds of the military men. A gun would be needed to effect entry into the Hall, it would have to be brought up from Athlone which was eighty miles away, and time was short for adequate preparations to be made to ensure complete success. So, before expressing a definite opinion, Colonel Cowan told the Lord Lieutenant that he would like to consult the police, the General Staff and Price, the Military Intelligence Officer. A further meeting was, therefore, fixed for ten o'clock that night and, while the Army officers consulted, Nathan dined with his guests in the Under-Secretary's Lodge and watched the children stage a play. Wimborne, for his part, being determined to see the business through, countermanded the arrangements that had been made for an official visit by him to Belfast the following day.

At ten o'clock the full conference convened in the Viceregal. Nathan was there and Edgeworth-Johnstone and Price, and, for the Army, Cowan, Lewis and a Captain Robertson. The Lord Lieutenant expounded his thesis that an attack on Liberty Hall, unaccompanied by the arrest of the leaders, would be not merely futile but provocative; that the stolen gelignite would have been removed; that the building itself was nothing without its occupants; and that of the two actions the arrest of the leaders was by far the more important. He wanted from sixty to one hundred of them locked up *that night*. Nathan did not agree. They would have to be careful that what they did was legal and to be certain that whatever charge was preferred could be sustained; if the ground of action was hostile association the concurrence

86

of the Home Secretary would be needed. This was the cautious Civil Servant speaking, remembering perhaps the heads that had rolled over the Bachelor's Walk affair. But Wimborne would have none of this; the criminals could be arrested and remanded until the concurrence of the Home Secretary was forthcoming. He offered to sign the warrants himself and to take full responsibility. He argued that the systematic disarming of six or seven hundred of the prominent rank and file of the Volunteers in Dublin was called for but he recognized that a large-scale operation of that sort was impossible that night. What was possible was to arrest a hundred known men. However, the result of the discussion was agreement that Easter Monday would be a bad day to make a raid on Liberty Hall with the city full of Volunteers and holiday makers; so the raid and the other action contemplated was postponed pending the result of Nathan's approach to the Chief Secretary and the preparation of a list of the men to be arrested. The meeting broke up at eleven-thirty.

On Easter Monday morning (24 April) Nathan walked over to the Viceregal Lodge. Estelle was with him. He was grave and hinted to her of trouble. She left him at the entrance as he went in to talk to the Lord Lieutenant. He did not stay long before going on to the Castle. According to his diary he got there at ten, and between that and noon he was with Price, the Intelligence Officer, who handed him a note he had just received from somebody whose name was written down as Hull. But we imagine that this was a mistake and that the note was either from Captain (later Sir) Reginald Hall, Chief of Naval Intelligence at the Admiralty who, with Mr (later Sir) Basil Thompson, the Assistant Commissioner of the Metropolitan Police and Head of the Criminal Investigation Department, had already begun the lengthy interrogation of Casement in Scotland Yard, or from another man also called Hall, a Major of Military Intelligence, who was engaged on the same task. The contents of the note are unknown to us, but its importance will be seen later. Together Nathan and Price then discussed how to implement the decisions taken the previous night, and as Norway, the Secretary of the Post Office, was a key man in these plans Nathan phoned him and asked him to come over to the Castle. Meanwhile, up in the Viceregal Lodge, the Lord Lieutenant sat down to write to the Prime Minister. Nathan had told him that morning no doubt that authority had not yet come from the Chief Secretary to proceed with the searches and arrests; and Wimborne, more restive than usual even, was telling Asquith how he deplored the delay and hoped that no mischief would occur as a result of it. He had got so far when a frantic telephone message came in from the police. The worst had happened, just when they thought it averted.

CHAPTER ELEVEN

The Norways, on coming to Ireland, had first lived in South Hill, a house in the Dublin suburbs at the Stillorgan end of Merrion Avenue, but when Fred, one of their boys, died in 1915 from wounds received near Armentieres, they left the house because of its painful memories and went to stay in the Royal Hibernian Hotel in Dawson St. Norway stored away in his office in the G.P.O. some souvenirs of their dead son – his sword and colt automatic revolver and a few odds and ends. In the hotel they were in the middle of things, and quite close to the Mansion House where, following a meeting to protest against the deportation of the Volunteer Organizers, they had seen a procession form and march through the streets singing *Die Wacht am Rhein* and revolutionary songs. People were beginning to ask anxiously 'what next?', Mrs Norway told her sister in a series of letters that were subsequently published, but the Government looked on and smiled and her husband tore his hair. His evident anxiety communicated itself to his younger son, Nevil, for on Easter Saturday, he induced his father to take Fred's automatic out of the safe in his office, and, having cleaned it for him, and charged the magazine and four other clips, he gave it back to him saying 'Now you have thirty shots, and I feel happier about you.' On that same day they were invited to tea with friends in Bray but, just when they were leaving the Hibernian, Norway was called to the Castle by Nathan who told him that a prisoner of consequence had been taken in Kerry, and that some risk existed of an attempt at rescue as he was being brought to Dublin on his way to London. He did not mention his name nor did Norway ask, though he surmized that it must be Sir Roger Casement. Nathan hinted at military precautions in the South, and possible restrictions on the use of postal services by the public. He made no suggestion of impending danger so that Easter Sunday passed off calmly for the Norway family.

On Easter Monday morning Norway went down after breakfast to the Sackville Street Club which was a few yards beyond the G.P.O. There he read the papers and then went to his office, intending to write some letters before lunch. He was still in the midst of his first letter when the telephone rang, and Nathan spoke, asking him to go up to the Castle. He gave no reason, but Norway surmized the need for some such steps as had been suggested two days before. Norway locked his desk, gave the key of his room to the porter, who was the only person on duty, and left saying he would be back in half an hour. It was then ten minutes to twelve. At twelve the Sinn Féiners seized the building. All the officials were turned out except one female telegraphist who remained behind to nurse a wounded sergeant.(1) Norway never entered that room of his again, for within a week there was nothing left of the whole building but the walls.

Norway saw nothing unusual as he walked up to the Castle. He went straight to Nathan's office and found him with Major Price, the Army Intelligence Officer. He turned to Norway as he came in and told him there was serious trouble in Kerry, where a ship had been seized with German officers on board, and material for a rising. Casement, whom he then named, had been conveyed to London under guard with no attempt at rescue. The position was serious and he desired Norway to take immediate steps for denying the use of the telephone and telegraph services over large areas of Southern Ireland to all but military and naval use. Norway said that this was too important a matter to be settled verbally and that he must have it in writing. 'Very well,' Nathan said, 'you write out what you want and I will sign it.' Norway was just finishing the necessary order when a volley of musketry crashed out beneath the window. He looked up, startled, 'What's that?' he asked, 'Oh, that's probably the long promised attack on the Castle,' cried Nathan, jumping up and leaving the room, while Major Price shouted from the window to some person below and then ran off too. Norway waited a few minutes and then followed them downstairs to see what had happened. At the foot of the staircase he found all the messengers huddled together. They were frightened out of their wits. They had just seen the policeman at the gate shot through the heart.

Nathan and Price had got the gates of the Upper and Lower Castle Yard shut, and as the attack was not pressed home, they were able to collect the small garrison in Ship Street Barracks and to alert the Military Headquarters in the Phoenix Park and the Viceregal Lodge. Norway, wandering around, discovered Nathan with his storekeeper breaking open the armoury in the hope of arming the handful of constables of the Dublin Metropolitan Police who formed the Castle guard. There were some revolvers there, but no cartridges : so that the constables remained of little use. The Chief Superintendent of the D.M.P. whose office was in the Castle sent out an order immediately calling in at once 'every available man, also cars and ammunition' but the response to this cannot have been very great; and a later order was probably superfluous which told the police to get off the streets. They had done so of their own initiative, for whenever they appeared in uniform they were fired on, with fatal effect in some instances. Another instruction in the midst of all the disorder to close the pubs injected some humour into the proceedings.

That afternoon when he could draw his breath Nathan telegraphed a summary of what had happened to Birrell :

'Insurrection broke out at noon today in Dublin when attack made on Castle but not pressed home. Since then large hostile parties has (sic) occupied Stephen's Green and various parties have held up troops marching from barracks firing on them and on houses. City Hall, Post Office, Westland Row station occupied by Sinn Féiners. Some railway bridges blown up and telegraphic communications generally interrupted. Have information of two policemen, one officer and half a dozen soldiers killed but casualties may be much more numerous. Situation at present not satisfactory but understand troops now beginning to arrive from Curragh.'(2)

But Birrell already had this story. Having got Nathan's cipher message of the 23rd decoded he wired from the Irish Office his agreement with the proposals to arrest and intern the Sinn Féin leaders. 'I then went to the Home Office', he said, 'and saw

Troup* – also Mr Basil Thompson† of Scotland Yard who has the case in hand. Then in comes Lord French (when I got back here) with startling news from Dublin – "Seizure by the Sinn Féiners of the Post Office" – "some railway stations" – "no streets safe" – but as the wires are cut no connection is possible and so no detailed news reaches me. It all fits in with the *man from Tralee* – and also with the enclosed telegram from New York which was in my Cabinet pouch *this morning*!' (This was a cable received by the Foreign Office (23 April) from Sir Cecil Spring Rice at Washington, indicating that among the papers seized by the police at New York were indications of a plan for gun-running in Ireland, not to begin before 23 April. Detachments of men were subsequently to be landed by the German Fleet and Zeppelins were to make a demonstration.)(*3*) 'But I am curious', Birrell went on, 'to know whether, in your opinion, what has happened in *Dublin* is the result of temper *after* failure to effect a landing or whether it really was the Rising contemplated in conjunction with the proposed landing. Until I know more as to how serious the Rising has been, I can say little. Lord French has men (and trains) to send you military assistance if required but with Friend's men, the D.M.P. and the R.I.C. I should expect you have enough for all your needs. Tomorrow I may be questioned in Parliament. Send me a *curt* reply to Ginnell's rigmarole. T. W. Russell‡ is crossing tonight and will tell me what happened. I must be ready with some *replies* and if the wire remains cut shall be in some difficulty. There is sure to be a howl – "I told you so." '(*4*)

The Sinn Féiners, or rebels as they were now also called, had the city more or less to themselves on Easter Monday. They could have ranged where they liked but they concentrated instead on barricading the important buildings they had seized and on a limited posting up of the Proclamation of the Irish Republic they had declared. From the handsome Post Office, which Norway had left so short a while before, the Union Jack was hauled down and the Irish green flag sent to the masthead in its place. The building in fact was rushed shortly after Nor-

* Sir Edward Troup, Permanant Secretary to the Home Office.
† Assistant Commissioner of Metropolitan Police and Head of C.I.D.
‡Irish Liberal M.P., Vice-President of the Irish Department of Agriculture and Technical Instruction.

way had left it, and his own elegant room appropriated for the rebel headquarters. The guard of soldiers at the door of the Instrument Room, the nerve centre of the telegraph system, did their best to keep the invaders at bay, but for some disciplinary reason which was never explained to Norway, they had been deprived of ammunition without his knowledge. Their rifles being empty, all they could do was to retreat inside the room and barricade the door. But the rebels fired through the door, shot a soldier in the face and forced the guard to surrender. Norway observed that had he not been rung up by the Under-Secretary, he should have been the only man armed on the premises. 'What then should I have done?' he mused, 'I presume I ought to have tried to hold the staircase, and keep the mob down. I hope I should have done so. The certain result would have been that I should have been shot at once, and the probable result would have been that the Government in London would have declared the whole trouble to have arisen from my wicked folly in firing on a body of peaceful, if armed citizens. So much one sees clearly, for politicians in a difficulty are never fair, and still less generous, but all else is dark.'

But for the moment the situation in which he found himself was dangerous enough. Behind the closed gates of the Castle he was a prisoner, as were Nathan, Price and the Solicitor General, afterwards Sir James O'Connor, with no force nearer than the Curragh to restore them to freedom. The rebels had posted snipers in the upper windows of houses commanding the exits, and were firing on anybody who tried to leave. It was, Norway reflected long afterwards, perhaps a worthwhile experience for a man like himself who had led a very sheltered life to become suddenly one of a besieged garrison, but he did not relish it at the time, and the disquiet of the situation was not much relieved by the fact that no attack developed, and that the sounds of fighting were still distant. He remembered drawing Nathan's attention to the fact that the small courtyard up and down which they were pacing was commanded by the windows of houses accessible from the street, and could not be considered safe. Nathan could not but agree, but as there were no soldiers to occupy those houses, they must take their chance. Why the Castle was not attacked Norway did not know but the prospect of this happening waned as the afternoon wore on; and at dusk a battalion of the South Staffords marched in having come up by train from the Curragh, and losing seven men – so Nathan was told – on the way over from the Kingsbridge terminal. 'Besieged we may not have been', said Norway, 'in a true sense; but the relief with which we watched the cheerful smiles of officers and men as they stacked their arms in the lower courtyard was considerable, for it is clear enough that the rebels could have made us prisoners without loss, and the lot of prisoners during the rebellion was not always comfortable or even safe.

'Safe as we felt in the presence of our own troops there was enough in the streets of Dublin that night of wild passion and fierce hope to convince the most careless of us that the country stood on the edge of an abyss, and as darkness fell the thought recurred oftener than one wished that this outbreak was formidable, and might be timed to coincide with some German stroke, possibly an invasion – for if that was in fact impossible we had no assurance of it then. When it grew quite dark, the troops attacked the City Hall, at the gate of the Upper Castle Yard, which the rebels had occupied and barricaded. I stood in the Lower Yard with the Solicitor General, listening to the noise of fighting. The rifle volleys came in crashes, mingled with the tapping of machine guns, and the shattering burst of bombs, so near that they seemed close beside us. The Yard was lit by torches, and crowded with men and soldiers, among whom from time to time a woman was carried in, caught in the act of carrying ammunition to the rebels, and fighting like trapped cats. It was a strange and awful scene. I turned to the Solicitor General and said, "This seems to be the death knell of Home Rule." Now he was a sane and moderate nationalist. But he said "Upon my soul, I don't know are we fit for it after all." And then, after a little interval, "The man I am sorry for is John Redmond."

'It was late before the noise of fighting died away, and not till after midnight did I prevail on the soldiers at the Castle gate to open it sufficiently to let me slip out and whisk around into a side lane, expecting to get a sniper's bullet between my shoulders as I ran. But nothing happened and I got back safely to the Royal Hibernian Hotel in Dawson Street, where my wife waited for me in considerable anxiety.' She had walked down town with Nevil with the intention of joining her husband for lunch;

94

but on seeing crowds gathering in Sackville Street outside the G.P.O. Nevil sent her home and went towards his father's club to see if he was there. On his way back he saw a troop of Lancers escorting some horse-drawn wagons coming down the street from the north end towards the Post Office, unaware at first apparently of what was going on, and then unsure as to whether they could continue on their way. They then decided to do so and when they were opposite the building, they came under fire from the rebels who killed four of them. These were the first men Nevil had ever seen killed. That afternoon, when they learned that all was quiet in Sackville Street, he induced his mother to go down to see the G.P.O. with him. The Secretary's room where some of the things they valued most in the world were stored appeared not to have been touched, and there were no men at the window. Next day, with his parents safe in the hotel, Nevil went off and joined a scratch First Aid unit as a stretcher bearer. He enjoyed himself immensely, and when the hostilities were over he received a parchment commending his gallantry in tending to the wounded at great personal risk.

Mrs Norway was invaluable in the trying days that followed. With her husband and one of his principal clerks, J. J. Coonan, who managed somehow to reach the Hibernian every day, they tried to function as a Post Office. They were helped conspicuously by Gomersall, the Superintending Engineer, who energetically directed the reconstitution as far as possible of the internal and external telegraph and telephone services by his staff of engineers, most of whom appear to have turned up regularly for duty at Aldborough House. Gomersall and his men drove round the outskirts of the city, picking up the ends of cables and leading them into Amiens Street through private circuits which they commandeered for the purpose, and this they did with such success that the adverse effect of the loss of the Telegraph Office in the G.P.O. was neutralized. The Telephone Exchange in Crown Alley was also in the Government's hands. But without exception there was no post office, apart from the room which Norway had commandeered at the Hibernian Hotel, and the telephone line which he had appropriated. At that telephone, he and his wife sat from early morning to late night.

It was a harassing job, and the Government were not very considerate. On Tuesday night they had just gone to bed when

Norway was called to the phone and told to go at once to the Viceregal Lodge. 'So he dressed', said his wife, 'and tried every way to get a motor; but of course no motor would go out. After some delay he got the ambulance of the Fire Brigade at Dr Wheeler's suggestion; but when it came, the men told Hamilton that they had been carrying the wounded all day, that they had been constantly stopped by pickets and the car searched, and that if they went and the car was stopped and found to contain Hamilton, they would undoubtedly all be shot; so Hamilton considered it too risky and it had to be abandoned. Eventually His Excellency gave his instructions over the phone in French, but that particular phone did not speak or understand French, so eventually he took the risk of the phone being tapped and gave them in English. At last Hamilton got to bed about 1 a.m. to be at the phone again at 5 a.m.'

Shortly after breakfast the police rang him up by direction of the Under-Secretary, and asked him to go to the Castle. Norway asked by what route. 'By Dame Street,' was the answer, 'that's quite safe today.' Norway was surprised, but to Dame Street he went and was just turning into it opposite Trinity College, when a shower of bullets swept down the streets, evidently from rebel rifles, and was answered by sharp successive volleys from Trinity College. He reached the Castle nevertheless by devious back lanes and found that Nathan had nothing to say to him which could not have been said over the telephone, without calling him away from the only point at which he could be of service, or exposing him to the very real risk of the streets. On the next day, knowing, Norway said, that his only substitute at the telephone was his wife, Nathan summoned him to the Castle four times 'without any reason of real advantage'.

Norway got a sample of the dangers that were abroad when he set off one morning for Gomersall's house at Terenure. Gomersall had incurred some risk a few hours before in coming to see him at the Hibernian and Norway thought it unfair to bring him in a second time. We have his own description of what happened. 'I went up Grafton Street,' he recorded, 'to the corner of St Stephen's Green, whence looking up towards Harcourt Street I could see a barricade of upturned motors etc., about half way along the Green, near the College of Surgeons. There was a brisk exchange of rifle and machine gun fire going

'NATHAN THE UNWISE'

Sir Matthew Nathan – Under Secretary for Ireland

British cavalry during the state entry of the Viceroy, Lord Wimborne, into Dublin Castle in 1914

DUBLIN CASTLE – CENTRE OF BRITISH RULE
The Upper Gate, showing the guardroom on the right

IRELAND'S RULERS

Sir Matthew Nathan and Augustine Birrell together in 1916

AFTERMATH

Scene of devastation around the G.P.O., which was the rebel
headquarters. Only a matter of days before this photograph
was taken the rebel flag flew over the building

AFTERMATH
Sackville Street and Eden Quay

The G.P.O. cannot be seen but it is on the left of Nelson's column (which is on left of picture)

DRAMATIS PERSONAE

Top row (*left to right*) : General Sir John Maxwell; John Dillon, Irish Nationalist leader; Augustine Birrell, Chief Secretary for Ireland. *Bottom row:* Lord Wimborne, Viceroy; Herbert Asquith, British Prime Minister; John Redmond, Irish National- list leader

on between the rebels entrenched at the further side of the Green
and our own soldiers in the Shelbourne Hotel, and with this
sound ringing through the air it was difficult to look trustfully
on a barricade though it seemed abandoned. I asked a few
people what the position was, and as they were assuring me the
fighting at that point was over, I saw a man walk through the
barricade towards us. If he could pass, it was clear that I could;
so I went on and entered Harcourt Street, which was the direct
and only way to Terenure. I had not gone far, however, when
the whole street was blocked by a flood of people swept back by
soldiers, and finding it impossible to go on, I turned again into
Stephen's Green and walked back the way I came. As I drew
near the College of Surgeons, I noticed several windows broken
by rifle bullets and at the same moment a bullet flew past my
nose and broke a window on my left. I then saw for the first
time that the College of Surgeons was held by rebels, and was
under heavy cross-fire from the Shelbourne Hotel. It was in fact
the command of the virago, the Countess Markievicz, and I was
at that moment crossing the line of fire.'

Norway set the uncertainties of life in Dublin those days
against a proposal that Nathan made to him towards the end
of the week. As usual there was a phone call and Norway was
asked to go down to the Castle. 'When I arrived', he said, 'he
wanted to know from me whether I could not restore postal
services over at least some part of the area of Dublin. I asked,
"What part?" "That is what I want you to tell me." "But how
can I?" I asked, "I have no official information whatever, and
no staff, as you are aware. You, on the other hand, as head of
the civil government of Ireland have full reports of police and
perhaps of military. Surely, I might ask you to indicate the
districts which you think safe enough to justify me in putting
postmen in uniform on the streets." "It is useless to ask me
that," he said, "for that is what I want from you." "I must press
upon you", I said, "that I have no means whatever of forming
a sound opinion. Will you not at least give me the reports you
have, and let me study them?" "No," he said, "I want your
sole judgement, and I want it in writing by four o'clock." I protested that this was scarcely fair, but in vain. Finding it was impossible to move Sir Matthew I returned to my hotel, and had
scarcely reached it when the Lord Lieutenant rang me up and

97

put the same question. Half an hour later the Irish Office in London pressed the same point on me, and it seemed obvious that the Government, being pressed in the House of Commons, wanted to get up and declare that the Rising in Dublin had been exaggerated, that some degree of order was restored and that postal deliveries had been resumed over considerable areas of the city. The fact that the rebels were firing on anyone who wore uniform, even the Fire Brigade, and that the postmen would certainly have been shot, was either unknown to them or treated as of no importance. To me it was the governing consideration. I had no member of my staff to consult with. But the case seemed clear. I rang up the mail cart contractor, and asked him whether he felt justified in sending out his vans and drivers into any part of Dublin. He said, rather indignantly, "You must know the answer to that question. Why do you put it to me?" "Because it is pressed on me," I said, "may I take it that you will not send out the vans?" "You may," he answered. I then wrote a short report to the effect that having been asked for my opinion as to the practicability of resuming postal services over some part of Dublin, and having at my command no official information about the state of the city, I could only say that my own observation led me to the conclusion that no such steps were practicable at the time, and that the lives of postmen would be in great danger if they appeared on the streets. I therefore declined respectfully to order them to go out. I took this myself to Sir Matthew Nathan, who received it ungraciously, not concealing his opinion that my attitude was obstructive. I had not, nor have I now, the least doubt that I was right.'

Norway thought that Nathan's manner and actions were those of a rather bewildered man. This did not surprise him for it was manifest, he said, that Nathan, as permanent head of the Irish Service and responsible adviser of Mr Birrell the Chief Secretary, was to blame for neglecting to suppress dangerous associations and for giving his confidence to men like John Dillon who did not deserve it. His intercourse with Dillon might have been imposed on him by Birrell, but if this was so, he considered it improbable that Nathan would have exercised his own judgement on the point at all, for that would have run counter to his conception of loyalty which he had expounded more than once to Norway – a conception differing vitally from

that traditional in the civil service, which enjoined that the pol-
tical head should always know what his chief advisers thought.
Norway endorsed what Lord Buxton, as Postmaster General had
said to him once, 'What I want from you is to give me your
best opinion. I may reject it but I always want to know it.'
Nathan's view, on the other hand, was that his duty lay in finding out what his chief wished him to do, and in helping him to
do it without discussion. Any degree of contention or discussion
even was, in his opinion, disloyalty.

Norway had availed of an opportunity on the very first day
of the Rising to let Nathan know that he had misread the signs.
They were sitting together during the afternoon when a constable brought in one of the proclamations that the rebels were
posting up in the city. Sir Matthew, when he had perused it,
passed it across the table for Norway to see. 'I had in mind',
Norway said later, 'the latest report sent to me from the Intelligence Department in the Castle, by Nathan's orders, and especially the assertion in this report that the I.R.B. was probably
dormant, and might be regarded as negligible. I put my finger
on the paragraph

"Having organized and trained her manhood through her
secret revolutionary organization, the Irish Republican
Brotherhood . . . and supported . . . by gallant allies in Europe
. . . she (Ireland) strikes in full confidence of victory."

and passed it back to Sir Matthew with the remark : "It seems
that the I.R.B. is not so dormant after all." Sir Matthew smiled
uncomfortably, but said nothing.'

Rooms had to be hurriedly abandoned inside the Castle so as
to meet the requirements of the military, and Nathan allowed
himself to be put away in the stables. It was in these crude
quarters that he was found on the Wednesday by Headlam, the
Treasury Remembrancer, who had managed, not without considerable difficulty, to reach the Castle from the country where
he had been spending the Easter holiday. He came via Stephen's
Green and at the edge of the railings there was a dead Sinn
Féiner and some young men were talking about giving him a
decent burial when an old woman screamed : 'Let the carrion
rot, bringing disgrace on the fair name of Ireland.' When he got

to the Castle he went first to his own office in the Lower Yard. 'It was bright sunlight and the soldiers were sitting with their rifles, smoking peacefully, against the wall of the houses at right angles to the terrace of my office. Occasional bullets, coming as I afterwards found, from Jacob's biscuit factory which the Sinn Féiners had taken, whined over their heads, but no one seemed to be replying to the fire. My office keeper . . . was rather flurried. He said that his children – he lived below my office – were much frightened : a Sinn Féiner had been killed by the soldiers on the roof of the office and not taken away. . . . He told me that the Under-Secretary was in the stable block, the buildings against which the soldiers were sitting, under cover from the firing from Jacob's. I went to the door and asked for the Under-Secretary whom I found busily writing, as usual, and quite calm. He gave me no information about the origin of the outbreak, said reinforcements were on the way and that it would soon be over, but that there would be no possibility of work for a day or two. . . .'(5)

One might wonder what Nathan was busy about in the strange circumstances in which he found himself. His papers show that as far as he could he continued to be the connecting link between the Administration in Dublin and the Government in London. He kept a continuous stream of telegrams flowing to the Irish Office summarising the situation as he found it every few hours and supplying such material as he could muster to answer the questions that were being raised in Parliament. Among the particular matters he mentioned were the capture on Easter Tuesday morning of the City Hall as a safeguard for Dublin Castle, the clearance of Stephen's Green, the partial destruction of Liberty Hall by naval guns, the rumours of a strong Sinn Féin force moving from Athenry towards Athlone which the G.O.C. said he could do nothing about until Dublin had been dealt with, and the necessary slowness of house to house fighting. He had to explain this to the Prime Minister who was anxious for quick results, and by way of illustration of the difficulties Nathan mentioned the opposition that the reinforcements from England had encountered on the road from Kingstown. The G.O.C. had asked for a further brigade from England and Nathan trusted it would be possible to send this without delay in order to end 'the present intolerable position'. In the middle of the week Nathan, at the instance of the Lord Lieutenant, took steps to publicize at home and in America the fact that Casement was a prisoner; this had hitherto been kept a secret. A telegram was sent in Beverley cipher to *Aftermath* who was to inform *Untoposy* that *Palladium* agents from Aurelia were in Ireland 'in order to influence *paginal*'. 'The cordial assistance of *Ambit* could be assured by giving its chief representatives in London exclusive news of the capture of an important person from Aurelia.' And the message ended: '*Balerric* unless Caddie' whatever that meant. The significance of the rest of the telegram was clear enough, however.

Among the papers that Nathan preserved was a copy of the Military Communique which announced that one of the principal leaders of the rebels P. H. Pearse,* 'was known to be inside the cordon suffering from a fractured thigh. A woman known as Countess Markievicz had also been seen, and another leader, James Connolly,† was reported killed ... Roger Casement had declared that Germany had sent all the assistance it was going to send: this was now at the bottom of the sea'. Another document was in the form of a Proclamation from Maxwell threatening to destroy all buildings in any area occupied by rebels – this was to be distributed through the priests so as to give women and children a chance of getting out. Nathan the same evening was in touch with the Lord Mayor about organizing citizens in committees to see to the burial of the dead. The police were out on the streets again in plain clothes, and picking up bits of information as to the condition of the rebels in the various areas. They conveyed to Nathan on Friday evening, the 28th, that a priest from Westland Row Church had been in touch with the 200 rebels barricaded in Boland's Flour Mills in Barrow Street and had advised them to give up; they had declined to do so, however, and said they were confident of winning.

But, in fact, the Rebellion was almost over, and Norway phoned from the Hibernian Hotel on Saturday, the 29th, to urge Nathan to have steps taken to prevent looting in the rooms of the G.P.O. 'There is probably still much of public value in the wreck, e.g. copper, and in various safes, some of which may be intact, there are material sums of money and other articles of

---

* This was unfounded.

† Connolly was wounded, and survived to be executed.

public and private importance.' He was thinking of his boy's things. He asked that access be given to the ruins and other places in Sackville Street to himself and other members of his staff, and that the necessary passes be issued.

Next day, Sunday, 30 April, Norway at the Castle told Nathan that a new General Post Office would be required and agreed to let Nathan suspend Post Office servants in his name. The staffs were returning after an absence of some days and would be asked where they had been and what they had been doing. If the replies were unsatisfactory the police were to be called in. On that day the military asked Nathan for the services of the finger print expert with his apparatus, and Miss O'Brien, of the United Irish League office, sent some questions over to him from Jury's Hotel on behalf of Redmond. She wanted to know what the telephone password was for that day for without it nobody could use the 'phone; was it the case that 4 p.m. had been fixed for the voluntary surrender, after which the orders were to shoot out of hand – this she said had been suggested. She asked for the names of any Sinn Féin leaders killed in the fighting, taken prisoner or executed. In particular, she wanted to know what had become of the seven signatories of the Proclamation of the Republic; where were MacNeill and Hobson; and had Sheehy Skeffington been executed, as was being stated. Nathan replied that all he knew was that Jacob's factory which was the only position still held by the rebels had been called on to surrender by 3 p.m. As far as he was aware the principal Sinn Féin leaders had been captured but he had no information as to their having been brought to trial.

That day – the first since Easter Monday that he was able to make a diary entry – Nathan simply noted 'Letters to Dillon',(6) and Dillon, who had been isolated with his family all Easter Week in his house in North Great George's Street, gave such news as he had been able to gather to Redmond. He warned him to be extremely cautious about making any public statement and to remain in London for the present. 'If you were here you would be held more or less responsible for all done by the Castle and military authorities – whereas of course you would have no voice – at all . . . You should urge strongly on the Government the *extreme* unwisdom of any wholesale shooting of prisoners. The wisest course is to execute *no one* for the present . . . If there were shootings of prisoners on a large scale the effect on public opinion might be disastrous in the extreme. *So far* feeling of the population in Dublin is *against* the Sinn Féiners. But a reaction might very easily be created . . .'(7)

The entry for Monday, 1 May, in Nathan's diary marked the close of one of the most amazing chapters in Irish history: 'Castle Office 9–6 with half-hour off for luncheon and tea. Interviews with Sir John Maxwell at Military House, Chief Commissioner, Norway, Lord Chancellor, Governor of Mountjoy, Master of Rolls. Left the Castle for the first time for a week in the morning to see Sir J. Maxwell and in the afternoon to return to Lodge, spending an hour at Viceregal on way. While there Birrell received cypher accepting resignation, to be announced on Wednesday. He returns tomorrow. Dined by myself at home. Casualties to date: 14 officers killed, 29 wounded; 51 men killed, 281 wounded.'(8)

And that was the Easter Rising as the Civil Government saw it.

CHAPTER TWELVE

Estelle Nathan described her experience in a long letter to her husband which she started to compose at the beginning of the week, adding to it from day to day as she waited for an opportunity to post it.

On Easter Monday morning as she walked with Nathan towards the Viceregal Lodge, he had spoken rather gravely to her about Ireland. The previous night he had been out meeting military persons, but she gathered that these secret councils had nothing to do with what was about to happen in Dublin. From rumours she understood that there had been disturbances in the West; there seemed to be no cause for alarm as to the state of Dublin. So she spent the rest of that morning painting in the Furze Glen, about a mile from the Under-Secretary's Lodge. She had her two children Maude and Pamela with her and Mrs Greene's niece, Dorothy Stopford. They were walking homewards at one o'clock when they heard three guns. The children were alarmed but Estelle, knowing the Viceregal party was moving to Belfast, calmed them by saying that these must be salutes on their departure. They had nearly finished lunch when Captain Maitland, one of the Aides de Camp, rang up from the Viceregal Lodge. 'I am sorry to say the Sinn Féiners are out,' he said, 'Sir Matthew is besieged in the Castle. He is all right at present as we have spoken to him. They tried to rush the Castle, but luckily the police managed to close the gates in time. Troops have been sent for.' Captain Maitland then threw out the suggestion that they might leave the Park and make for somewhere else, but Estelle declined. Their anxiety grew, however, as what began as desultory firing developed into 'a big battle' and appeared to range around the Viceregal Lodge. They could see yellow-brown smoke rising above the trees and slowly form a heavy cloud. They heard afterwards that this was an attack on the Royal Barracks and that the Viceregal Lodge was all right.

That evening Matthew rang up to ask how they were and to tell them that he was, himself, quite well but unable to leave the Castle and would stay with the Kelly's who had quarters inside the walls. He did not go to bed that night, but lay down on the sofa for a short time. At the Viceregal the A.D.C.s did not go to bed either. About 10 p.m. they sent a soldier over to enquire how they were.

The Telephone Exchange was open for military messages only, but on Tuesday Estelle was able to get through to Matthew at the Castle and he gave her the news in French but said very little. The Castle, she gathered, was now strongly garrisoned, troops and artillery having poured in from the Curragh. They were not to send him any clothes or other things as he thought it wiser not, though the gardener thought he might be able to penetrate.

At mid-day Wednesday frequent firing could be heard and the question of supplies came up. 'One of the servants bicycles to a little shop at the Park gate, and of course we got no fish and I rather wonder how we are provisioned at all, but she seems to come back with plenty of food. She was warned by an officer not to go further: there is a machine gun trained across the road, and the trees are lined with troops.' About two o'clock a loud bombardment and much rifle firing was again heard, and this lasted until tea time. At that hour one of the staff came in badly scared. He had been down past the Phoenix monument, and near the Polo grounds bullets were whistling across the road and the soldiers were calling to everyone to lie down flat. It all seemed rather near the Viceregal; and the servant told Estelle that a company of Lancers was now guarding the Under-Secretary's fence. 'I cross-examined him', Estelle wrote, 'before telephoning to the Castle, as we began to feel it might be better to decamp and he did not waver from his story, but the parlour maids both seemed to think him a bit of a coward, and that in any case the bullets were our own, and not Sinn Feine (sic).

'I had just settled that the matter was not as bad as he seemed to think when two terrific explosions occurred quite near, followed by musket firing. The explosions appeared to be between us and the Viceregal and we saw blue smoke rising between us, just beyond their boundary wall. I felt things were getting warm and telephoned to the Castle to enquire what we should do. We were advised to remain quiescent and Matthew promised to telephone General Friend and let us have details of what was happening. Nerves were rather overstrained so I had to read Sherlock Holmes very steadily to the children for an hour. He is a great resource. Pamela feels it all very much, and always tries to shut herself into a room and become absorbed in a book or game and try and forget. Maudie is thrilled at living through such an exciting crisis and thinks more of the interest than the horror. Pam says "it is most unpleasant". She was quite upset the first evening and when I said it was like a Zeppelin raid, she said, half sobbing : "But it is much worse. Because it is in the Empire", and that seemed thoughtful. She was anxious about Matthew's food etc., but has been reassured on that point.'

That evening Lord Basil Blackwood, the Lord Lieutenant's Secretary, rang up and told them not to worry about the bullets that had been 'spinning about and the extremely near explosion. No damage had been done; it was a shrapnel shell of our own which fell and burst where it was not meant to do, and the bullets were also from our own somewhat excited young soldiers ...' Later on Matthew came on the phone again and Estelle asked him if they were protected in any way as there were moments when they felt rather defenceless. He said they were now well taken care of. There were more police about than one would imagine, as they were not wearing uniform they would have been shot in the town if they had appeared. Matthew was going to bed that night but was expecting Mr Birrell who had started in a torpedo boat. 'Everything is known in England whereas owing to the absence of papers and letters we are in ignorance. Matthew said the business was now a series of Sidney Street incidents and houses had to be bombarded to get the Sinn Féiners to surrender. . . .'

On Thursday he phoned again. He had slept well when he once got to bed and had seen Mr Birrell. He sounded more confident. They were to expect to hear heavy guns again that day; but in fact the day was comparatively quiet, and the sound of guns and rifles less frequent. 'The day seemed long, though the whole morning was taken up over an examination paper we set ourselves, "The Phoenix Park College", and the

children were intensely amused at their own and our great wit
. . . The weather was beautiful and we spent all the day in the
garden.'

Friday was equally fine, though colder, and more desultory
firing was heard. 'Matthew has had a bad cold and has suffered
from only having ladies' small handkerchiefs and a want of warm
clothing on his bed. We have today been able to send him a bag
and two rugs . . . He enquired about food as there is now a military cordon round Dublin and the food question is giving cause
for thought . . .' Estelle found when she enquired in the kitchen
that supplies were running low. No meat had come since Saturday, nor any bread, and that morning the milk had not been
sent. There was also a shortage of groceries and butter which
explained why they were being less lavishly treated. Estelle sent
the chauffeur off in the direction of Lucan on a bicycle and he
came back without meat, poultry and butter but with sufficient
groceries to last until Tuesday . . . 'The trouble now is sniping
from houses and we hear that even the women help in this, and
it is in this way that casualties occur.'

About six o'clock Estelle had a long talk with her brother-in-
law. He was grave and discussed the terrible food question. The
military cordon was preventing anything from coming in and
he said 'we could not hold out for more than 24 hours'. Later
that night Captain Murry Graham told her that there were
grave doubts as to the wisdom of the policy as of course the
suffering inhabitants would side against the military. 'Just as
we were finishing dinner Kearney announced Lady Frederick
Conyngham and mother . . . I found the two women quite ex-
hausted and terrified, having fled from their place, Lagore,
twelve miles out owing to the Sinn Féin rising there. They had
seen one dead policeman and four wounded ones, and when
they left there was indiscriminate firing and a battle raging
within three miles of their house. They had been whisked away
in a car – only just in time. They had a terrible day – Lady
Freddy was a great friend of Her Excellency's and wanted to
telephone before going to the Lodge. She gave her message
about the rising near her house both to the Viceregal and to
Matthew, and it fell like a bomb upon them as the country was
supposed to be safe, and their excellencies had even contemplated sending their children to her. But the Viceregal was very

full and of course I immediately offered to put them up, so they remained with us that night . . .' Murry Graham came in to see them later; he was very depressed and gave them news of the fall of Kut and of the many casualties in Dublin. But, he promised them that on the next evening, Saturday, at five he would have cars and passes to get them to the mail boat at Kingstown by a detour of some thirty miles. All that Friday night the bombardment, rifle fire and the conflagrations continued with such excessive violence that Estelle could not sleep. Next day they packed, and at four o'clock in the afternoon just before they left, Matthew phoned the news that the rebels had surrendered. The armoured cars with mobile guns had hastened this. 'So we had to say goodbye very sadly over the telephone and left not having seen him since Monday, the morning of the Rising.' The journey to Kingstown was not without excitement. The car punctured twice and they were stopped by sentries and police at every crossroads and village. Everyone turned out in the villages and eyed them curiously. There were soldiers, officers and gun carriages; and more mules than they had ever seen in their life. They were led past a challenging officer every two or three yards into the mail boat. In this fashion, and much to their relief, they got safely back to England leaving Matthew to face the most disagreeable personal problem of his career.(1)

CHAPTER THIRTEEN

Lord French, who, we must remind ourselves, was Commander-in-Chief of the Home Forces, with his headquarters at the Horse Guards in London, received the news of the Rising from the Army in Ireland shortly after noon on Easter Monday. He directed the two brigades of the 59th division which were not in Ireland, to go there at once. One was at Liverpool and the other, the cavalry brigade, at Aldershot. A battery of guns and 10,000 hand grenades were sent over. He also placed the 60th division which was at Salisbury under orders, but before actually dispatching them, he told the Prime Minister, who had passed on Nathan's telegram to him, that he wanted to consult the General Staff. 'The Germans are, of course, prompting this Rising in Ireland', he said, 'to prevent us from sending reinforcements to France or to delay their dispatch. I do not want to play into their hands more than we can help.'(*1*) The Chief of the Imperial General Staff, Sir William Robertson, agreed with French that the situation in Ireland as they knew it at the moment did not necessitate the dispatch of another division; neither was there any reason to distrust the loyalty of the Irish regiments – six battalions of which were distributed between Cork, Kinsale and Fermoy – as had been suggested by Lord Midleton. French, to make himself *au courant* with the political situation, arranged a meeting with Redmond who came over from the House of Commons to see him. Redmond cannot have known at that time who exactly was behind the Rebellion; yet he seems to have felt it would consist of a combination of Sinn Féiners and Larkinites and he distinguished the former from what French's biographer says he described as 'some Independents under MacNeill in Dublin'. This combination, he told French, 'was neither numerous nor formidable', were not supported by any body of opinion in Ireland, and the population of Dublin was hostile to them. Nevertheless, he expressed the hope that great care would be taken by the military authorities in dealing with them because a good deal of street fighting might have to be undertaken and if innocent people were hurt to any great extent it might turn the popular feeling in favour of the rebels.(2)

The Government had made known through Kitchener, the Minister for War,(3) their wish that a General should be sent to take command and French decided on Sir John Maxwell, sent word to him, and arranged to see him early on Easter Tuesday morning to give him full instructions. Maxwell, by the time he had got a good staff together, did not get away until the afternoon of Thursday the 27th. He had been in Ireland a dozen years before as Chief Staff Officer to the Duke of Connaught; recently he had been in Egypt but had been recalled because, as he put it, 'the political people have got their knives into me'; and was actually recuperating after a spell in a nursing home when he was told he was wanted to stamp out an insurrection in Dublin that had placed the King's subjects in peril of their lives.

Meanwhile the Lord Lieutenant, revelling in his new-found importance, had written a long letter to the Prime Minister. He did this on Easter Tuesday, 25 April, and because he had suspended the mail service, the letter had to go by destroyer. In it he confirmed the optimism of the military, but took some pleasure, we fancy, in being able to say that the rebels were still investing the Castle 'where Nathan is held up' while serious street fighting continued and some looting. The insurgents were taking themselves seriously. 'I hear', he wrote, 'that they have raided the printing offices of the *Freeman's Journal*', which was alongside the G.P.O., 'and have given a receipt in the name of the Irish Republic. In fact, they have posted placards announcing a provisional republican government signed by their prominent members', and he sent a copy for Mr. Asquith to see. 'Paradoxically', he added, 'there sits in Steevens (sic) Green a throned queen – they say – Countess Markievitz (sic).'

Despite his sarcastic tone, Wimborne did not minimise what had taken place. The Rising did not miss success by much, he said, and was connected by a chain of evidence with enemy instigation and assistance. He had been obliged to proclaim martial law in the city and district of Dublin, and intended on the morrow to declare the Irish Volunteers and the Citizen Army illegal and dangerous associations. Later when order was restored, the military authority contemplated, with his concurrence, the systematic disarmament of the rebels and the arrest of a considerable number of their leaders. They proposed also to make an end of Liberty Hall and two other Sinn Féin arsenals. It was their duty and their opportunity to eradicate this evil. So far there had been no evidence of popular sympathy for the Rising, and they owed it as much to the loyal population as to themselves to exhibit determination. The King, to whom a copy of this letter was sent by the Prime Minister, 'read it with interest'.(4)

Birrell answered questions in an uneasy House of Commons on the 25th and 26th, and then travelled to Ireland by destroyer. As he landed at the Custom House wharf at six in the morning of Thursday, the 27th, he could hear firing on both sides of the river. He motored quietly through streets held by the cordon of soldiers to the Viceregal Lodge where he saw Wimborne and Friend. Nathan was still in his room at the Castle 'but could get out if he wanted to'. The difficulties of the situation were revealed to Birrell on the spot. Sackville Street, including the Post Office, and the Four Courts, with intervening parts of the city, were strongly held by the insurgents from houses by that time prepared for defence and barricaded. Snipers in civilian clothes were all over the city and having fired at the troops from windows and roof tops could discreetly walk out afterwards as peaceful citizens. 'Most elusive', he commented. It would be necessary, he told London, to employ artillery fire to demolish some of the houses to enable troops to assault the main position in Sackville Street. This was necessary because of the stubborn resistance of the rebels and to avoid heavy casualties among the troops. His information was that an unfavourable situation existed in the West and that more troops would be needed as soon as possible.

From then on the news was more reassuring. The officer commanding the Southern part of Ireland, General Stafford, described the situation there as quite satisfactory. He had disposed his available troops to meet any emergency and did not ask for more. All was quiet in the North, and it had been found possible to send a thousand soldiers down from Belfast during the night of 24/25th. Elsewhere such disturbances as had been reported were in three areas, in the Counties Wexford, Meath and Galway, but none of these was of real importance, and reinforcements were being sent. A thousand Royal Marines, who had put in at Queenstown with machine guns and twelve-pounders, had been diverted to Galway. It would appear that, irrespective of these marines and the 59th division, there were in Ireland at this time 17,000 infantry approximately, 3,149 cavalry and 1,000 artillerymen but these were all draft-finding units and third-line troops.(5)

General Friend had resumed his command in Dublin on Tuesday, 25 April, and as reinforcements began to reach him, he set about establishing a line of posts from Kingsbridge Railway Station to Trinity College which divided the insurgent forces into two and gave a safe line of advance to troops extending operations to the North and South, and permitted communication by despatch rider with some of the commands.(6) The divided insurgents were cut off, on the north side of the Liffey, in the strong points they held at the G.P.O. and the Four Courts and, on the southern side, their resistance was based on Boland's Mill (which covered the railway line out from Westland Row terminus) and on Stephen's Green, Jacob's Biscuit Factory and the South Dublin Union. To help in the task of reducing the insurgents, Dublin Castle and Trinity College were used as troop concentration centres in addition to the barracks on or close to the South and North Circular Roads. By the time Maxwell arrived on the morning of Friday, 28 April, and took over he found that Friend had the situation well and truly in hand. He praised him for his prevision and for his energetic and successful handling of the situation. By this time the rebels in Sackville Street were hemmed in all round and the position was ripe for the taking.

On the 28 April also Birrell got down to the Castle; it was not by any means, he said, a joy ride. He found that Campbell, the Attorney General, O'Connor, the Solicitor General and Nathan had reached the view he himself already held that it would be unwise, there being no immediate military necessity, to extend martial law to the whole of the country. By telegraph, he had already given his reasons for so thinking to the Prime Minister and he now added by letter that universal martial law would have an indirect effect on the Nationalists throughout Ireland. 'I don't place too much confidence in them, although I am sure that they won't tar themselves with the Sinn Féin brush just now, but it would be a pity to give them any excuse for holding aloof from the Government whilst engaged in the effort of crushing the rebellion.' At this point, Birrell raised the question of his own position. 'Of course', he told Asquith, 'all this shatters *me*. The Thing that has happened swallows up the things that might have happened had I otherwise acted.' And as the motor waited to take him on another 'joy ride' he left himself unreservedly in the Prime Minister's hands.(7).

The next morning (Saturday, 29 April) Birrell was again at the Castle and his sense of humour was touched when he found 'the Food Committee (despite its name) doing good work in the distribution of food'. Food was not scarce, but getting the food into back streets, and negotiating the military cordon, that was the difficulty. Meanwhile, the Prime Minister had supported the military view that there should be general martial law and the proclamation had been issued; it was not easy, however, Birrell told him, in any but a technical sense to *publish* it broadcast. 'The great thing is to spread the news of the impending collapse in Dublin. This will be worth more than all the proclamations in the world. Except indeed one which the General has already issued warning all inhabitants in named areas in Dublin to clear out.'

That the Rising was about to collapse was apparent. Birrell, confirming what was already known in London by that time, told Asquith that Pearse, 'the wretched "Commandant" of the insurgents', had been before the General at the Military Head-quarters in Parkgate Street and that this had followed Maxwell's tactic of keeping the engagement going all the previous night reducing the enemy to despair. The General anticipated that 'the whole pack of them' would unconditionally surrender at nightfall. The General Post Office was evacuated, but a ruin, and on the verge of giving in was the Four Courts, which Birrell described as containing the Great Seal and 'all the historical records of Ireland since the day Henry the Second was foolish enough to do what the Romans never did, cross the Irish Channel. If this proves true', he went on, 'it will be an enormous relief, as I feared that those who were left of the rebels might get possessed of houses in the suburbs ... and keep it up again after a desultory but dangerous fashion for a good time'. Certain districts in the provinces had been 'very jumpy' but the news would take the heart out of the boldest rebels. 'The quiet of Kerry seemed to point to some hope of a German landing but I think now we can destroy that last lingering hope. The horrible thing proves how deep in Irish hearts lies this passion for insurrection'. He stressed that there were a great many young people in it. It was a shattering blow to a great deal of 'political stuff', but it would not get rid of it. And then as he hurried to get the Bag he returned once more to his personal dilemma. 'Let me know what you expect me to do'.(8) And on the following day, 30 April, Birrell wrote this, his last letter from Ireland:(9)

Secret

Viceregal Lodge,
Dublin.
Sunday, 3 o'clock

My dear Asquith,

I have just come back from the Castle. There is still firing going on – round Jacob's Biscuit Factory – in a *crowded* situation but it is now surrounded and can't hold out long. The *Four Courts* are evacuated and no great damage has been done. Men (many of them boys) are surrendering freely, tho' one Leader has repudiated the *'Commandant'*. I have seen many of the prisoners, a miserable lot they looked, unfit for *street* fighting, but under shelter of the houses dangerous and hard to dislodge. Those who have been interrogated suggest that they expected Casement to be in Dublin – but not much so far has been extracted from them. Some say 'I thought it would be a good "shew" '. The leaders, both fighting leaders and stump-orators, are criminals to whom short shrift should be given. A great haul of prisoners has been made today, and I hear that some of the instigators and inspirers of this mad revolt are taken. A great many *young* fools from the National *University* ! are amongst them. It is a small combination of the old Physical Force Party, one or two Labour men like James Connolly, now in the Castle *badly wounded*, and idealistic youths sick of the *Freeman's Journal*, plus an *idle* crowd who have made this Revolution. You get much better news from Headquarters than any I can give, so

I regard myself only as a supernumerary. An important point not yet capable of ascertainment is the number of persons actively in the Dublin insurrection. It is being whittled down from 8,000 to little over 1,000. 3,000 is probably the outside number *counting all sorts*. The news from the country shews that the news of surrender, widely circulated, has and is having its inevitable effect. Retirement is the order of the day. *Meath,* where the worst has been, has been reached today by soldiers who if they *could* have been sent earlier it would have been better – but I daresay they couldn't. They will squash it any moment (?). Enniscorthy – where they had put up a fight – is surrendering unconditionally – so I have just heard by wire. I expect by Tuesday it will be as *an Insurrection* over. The casualties, though horrible to reflect upon so far as the soldiers and constables are concerned, will not be large in themselves. The English newspapers are scandalous. After Dublin is settled with, the country Sinn Féiners will be 'collected'. The police can give *in each locality* a full list. Though some will or may escape through the meshes, many will be caught. Disarmament . . .* will be more difficult but must be attempted. Maxwell has an idea (after dealing with the Leaders) and after sending his hordes across to Holyhead or somewhere in that neighbourhood to be confined in camp to offer them the choice of the Trenches. How far that will recommend itself to the War Office I cannot say, nor what chance there would be of the offer being accepted.† I have had no direct communication with Redmond or Dillon. They will watch the proceedings of the Military *after* the rebellion is put down very closely. It is not an *Irish* Rebellion – it would be a pity if *ex post facto* is became one, and was added to the long and melancholy list of Irish Rebellions.

I don't know (tho' I can partly guess) how things political stand in London. I half suspect that I should have been back (tho' in what capacity is another and indifferent matter) in my place in Parliament on *Tuesday* but that seems now a little *premature* – and as I have to consider not only my own *position* hereafter but Nathan's and Friend's as well as the

---

*The sense of a passage here in parenthesis is not clear.

†Asquith killed this idea (Gerald French, *Life of Field-Marshal Sir John French,* London, 1931, p. 340).

Lord Lieutenant's. I must be more circumspect in speech than otherwise, were I alone in the business, I should be at any great pains to be. You will I am sure *let me know* (as quickly as possible) what you wish me to *do* in the general interest of the country. I *fully appreciate my own position,* but am not in the least frightened of the House of Commons and can put up (for myself) a good fight – tho' I daresay the general verdict will be adverse, and of course I can't go on. It is the finest Easter I have ever known in my Nine Years which is ironical enough. I am very sorry for Nathan the *Unwise* – who up to Ireland had always been successful *everywhere.* Nobody can govern Ireland from England save in a state of siege. A good many 'loyalists' here are glad things have happened as they have, and look forward to a renewed . . .* of Protestant Ascendancy. I hope (against hope) that something better than this will eventuate from it. I am very sorry that just at this time I have increased the burden of your situation. I advised you to *pole-axe* me some months ago . . .†

In haste for Bag,
A. B.

The following day, 1 May, Asquith expressed his pleasure at the good progress that was being made and accepted Birrell's resignation 'with infinite regret'.(*10*) This was no formality. Between the two men something much deeper than friendship had existed for many years. Birrell could speak of his love for his chief and after their leave-taking he was so moved that he could not remember what Asquith had said to him. He knew, however, that the Prime Minister had 'wept and stood staring out of the window jingling some half crowns in his pocket'.(*11*) This was not the ending to his career Birrell had expected. He had wanted to go down in history as the last of the Chief Secretaries, which would have been the inevitable and desirable culmination of his work, and that of successive Liberal Governments, for Home Rule. But now he felt 'smashed to pieces' as

*Word illegible.
†Emotion and the need to catch the Mail boat made a final sentence partly illegible, but its drift is clear enough. Birrell was sick of the whole business.

the result of 'a supreme act of criminal policy' that was 'nothing more than a Dublin row'.(*12*) His departure gave rise to considerable rejoicing among Tory-minded officials.(*13*)

An outcome of the conversation with the Prime Minister was a cipher telegram from Birrell to Nathan asking for his resignation too (3 May). We have not got the cipher which must have been couched in unusual terms because in the letter which Birrell sent after it he said he felt *bound* to cypher Nathan as he did, because he knew him so well and 'a common misfortune makes one even more sensitive than usual – as to what one ought to do'. The Prime Minister had as yet, he said, no ideas of how to make his reconstruction, and it might be that he would find it impossible to do without Nathan. But what he had told him was what Asquith wanted at the moment. As for the Enquiry into the cause of the Rising which had been decided on, the Prime Minister did not know by whom or how it would be conducted; the War Office were already preparing their memoranda for it and Birrell supposed that Nathan and he should prepare theirs at once. 'We must collaborate together but I am afraid yours will be longer and more laborious than mine.' He ended – 'I was much touched by your parting with me and the way you felt it. I can assure you that since we have been thrown together I had taken greatly to you and admire and respect your character and great ability. Better to sink with some people than to go to the House of Lords with others'.

Nathan duly and dutifully wrote to the Prime Minister:

> Chief Secretary's Office
> Dublin Castle.
> 3 May 1916

Dear Mr. Asquith,

The attempt to keep order in Ireland during the war has failed and you will probably consider that I can no longer be usefully employed here. In acquiescing readily in this decision I would like to express my deep regret that I have not been able better to serve His Majesty's Government at this critical time and also my thanks for the kindness which you have always shown to me.

> Yours, sincerely,
> Matthew Nathan.

Asquith received this letter 'with much regret' and briefly expressed the Government's indebtedness but he had made up his mind that Nathan must leave Dublin and he urged him to come over to London as soon as he could conveniently leave. 'Nathan the Unwise' had no chance of being left behind. Nor did he complain on that score. Indeed he seemed quite prepared to shoulder responsibility for what had gone wrong. He told Birrell, for instance, that it was depressing him more and more to think of the injury that had come to him from placing in him the confidence of which he was so proud,(14) and he told Friend how sorry he was that his advice might have led at times to inaction which Friend might now regret.(15) But that was characteristic of Nathan. What we would like to think was uncharacteristic of Birrell was his labelling of Nathan as unwise; this might indicate a desire not to bear in private the responsibility he had to carry in public for what went wrong, or it may just have been the sort of literary quip he liked to indulge in. In Lessing's play *Nathan der Weise* a man noted for his wisdom is called on to choose from three rings, identical in appearance, the solitary genuine and valuable one. He does so successfully, whereas Sir Matthew Nathan, with such choices as were open to him, had fared less well.

However, as the Irish saying goes, there was a power of dry eyes at Nathan's dismissal. The Unionists had no regrets at his departure, though many of them put all the responsibility for what had happened on his Chief. The Irish Party insisted upon the resignation of the Irish Executive in toto. 'I am strongly of opinion', Dillon told Redmond, 'that, as Birrell is going, Nathan and Wimborne should also go. I am *strongly* against leaving Wimborne if the others go, and, much as I like Nathan in some respects, I feel quite clear that he can be of no further use in Ireland.' And he should go although he had behaved so splendidly; were it not for him the Castle would have been taken. For successors, Dillon suggested a strong military man as Lord Lieutenant, Lord French or Sir John Maxwell if he was a Home Ruler; Montague would be the best of a bad lot as Chief Secretary, and the Under-Secretary, although that could wait, should be someone nominated by the Irish Party. In fact they were ultimately not consulted about any of these appointments.(16) 'Evidently,' Dillon told Redmond, 'this Government think they can manage Ireland without taking any account of our opinions.'(*17*) The Nationalists had been the greatest sufferers in the Rising; their policy had gone completely awry and they must have begun to feel in their bones by now that it was only a matter of time until they passed from the political scene.

Nathan cleared up his papers and packed his bags but, despite the haste in getting him out of Dublin, he overlooked nothing in the process. In the last day or two a thousand special constables were needed, watchers placed on the Ports, the dead disposed of, and the people who had behaved well during the emergency 'recognised'. Norway's department shone out brilliantly among these, particularly the staff at the Telephone Exchange, the telegraphists at Amiens Street and the engineers. These men and women had worked day and night and had played a considerable part in bringing the 'disturbances' so quickly to an end. The rebels had failed noticeably to disrupt the communications services on the Easter Monday despite much preparation and inside knowledge. They had taken the Central Telegraph Office in the G.P.O. but not the main Telephone Exchange in Crown Alley; so that at no stage were the Government without internal and external lines of communication, and from this point of view the situation rapidly improved as the week wore on.(*18*)

Nathan did not omit the formality of tendering his resignation officially to the Lord Lieutenant, although it cannot have been easy for him to do so. He expressed his sorrow that Wimborne should have to think that the confidence he had placed in his judgement, sometimes against his own, should have been ill-placed, and said he was taking from Ireland with him a great burden of regret, which, however, had 'no personal cause'. His last days in Dublin were strenuous, working from early morning till late in the evening, and interviewing among others, Sir John Maxwell and John Dillon.

The leaders of the Rising were being court-martialled and he told Maxwell that it was very important from the point of view of future quiet that he should be able to send Dillon a reassuring note from him as to the general lines on which the courts-martial were working and to tell him that the particular cases he had brought to notice would be enquired into. Dillon had been protesting strongly. He was afraid that the English military officers were determined to have a slaughter on their hands. The

Irish Times had been crying out savagely for their blood. And with Birrell gone and Nathan going, there was only Wimborne left on the civil side and Dillon had no confidence in him in a business of this kind.(*19*)

On the day Nathan left, Friday 5 May, he was at his desk until 6.15 p.m. and then went to Kingstown where he was seen off by his assistant O'Farrell. Appropriately in the circumstances he had 'a rough passage'. But when he got to London next morning he worked from 9.15 till 11.45 and then for the next two and a half hours he was closeted with the Prime Minister, Birrell and Sir Robert Chalmers who, it had been announced, was to succeed him temporarily in Ireland. He lunched with Birrell in the New University Club and the conversation turned largely on what they were going to say to the Royal Commission of Enquiry that had now been announced. Birrell wrote him the following day (Sunday 7 May) offering a few ideas. The Enquiry, he presumed, would call evidence, and a grand volume of evidence would be proferred and would have to be sifted and examined by the Commissioners. 'As to the actual condition of Dublin prior to the outbreak,' he said, 'we must consider what effect that evidence when sifted is likely to produce on the Tribunal and how best to put our case – both what we did do and what we didn't – the reasons for both action and inaction – before it with force and reason. In my opinion this is the crux of the case so far as we are concerned.'

In the circumstances it would have been the normally expected thing that all members of the Executive should resign, the Lord Lieutenant as well as the other two; and Asquith, under pressure, was inclined to think this also. But when Joseph Albert Pease, the Liberal Whip who had succeeded Hobhouse as Postmaster General and who had gone over to Dublin to see what had happened, broached the subject in the Viceregal Lodge, he got a very blunt reaction. Wimborne, quite understandably, saw no adequate reason why he should resign. Such action would be interpreted as a recognition on his part that he had been guilty of mismanagement and errors of judgement for which he was not responsible and for which he could not be held liable. Had his advice been taken and his suggestions accepted the events of Easter Week would have been averted, and he did not see how his position, as the King's representative in Ireland, would be strengthened, were he to offer to resign and thereby associate himself with the errors of judgement of which Birrell and Nathan had admitted themselves to have been guilty.(20) Nevertheless Wimborne received a message a couple of days later, through his Secretary, Basil Blackwood, that the Cabinet wanted his resignation, and he lost no time in giving it and in regretting the circumstances which had rendered it necessary. In view of the line he had taken with Pease it is difficult to understand why he should have added, as he did, how much he wished he had been a more efficient instrument in the promotion of these circumstances and thus to have been perhaps able the better to justify the appointment the Prime Minister had conferred on him. But then letters of Ministerial resignation usually conceal more than they reveal, and are often used by Governments for face-saving purposes. Asquith wired the next day thanking Wimborne for his letter which was greatly appreciated but asked him to remain on until further arrangements were made. It was this situation that Philip Hanson of the Board of Works said would be comic, if things were not so serious – a suspended Viceroy, a non-existent Chief Secretary and an Under-Secretary who was fresh to the country and apparently not going to stay.

The calls for resignation ended there but not the rumours of others to come. Ignatius O'Brien, the Lord Chancellor, wrote to the Prime Minister to tell him that more or less veiled suggestions were being freely made that he, as a member of the Irish Government, would have to share responsibility for what had happened, but he did not know whether the Prime Minister was aware that since the Coalition Government had come into office he had not been consulted in any matter of policy or government. The Prime Minister replied immediately. A Royal Commission was being set up, he said, to enquire into the circumstances in which the rebellion had occurred. Without prejudice to the future the Viceroy was being asked to resign and his office put *pro tempore* in commission. O'Brien could rely on him, Asquith, to safeguard his position should it be the subject of open or covert attack.

Pease, when reporting on Wimborne, gave the Prime Minister a summary of the Post Office situation. 'The burnt G.P.O. presents to the eye an imposing spectacle of what happens in the centre of a city when a battle is forced by 2,000 rebels. The walls all remain as a mere shell, everything inside was gutted except the safe, found intact with £7,000 inside and we only lost £60 in cash.' This was apparently the Accountant's safe; that in Norway's office perished, and with it the precious souvenirs of his son, Fred. A search was made in the rubble but nothing was found; and with that act Norway disappears from the scene, to reappear, after his retirement in due course from the Civil Service, as a writer of travel books and a commentator on Dante's *Divine Comedy*. It should be said, however, that he protested personally in London against the indiscriminate dismissal of men and women of his staff accused of participating in the Rising, and was instrumental in having a committee of enquiry set up which acted as a brake on the intentions of the military. Pease had told Asquith that the allegation that the Postal Service was honeycombed with Sinn Féiners would not on investigation prove accurate. This was true, and Friend was perhaps symbolizing his appreciation of what the loyal staff had done in restoring communications when he presented Pease with some of the well-designed republican postage stamps which the military had found and which proved how carefully thought out had been the preparations for the Rising.(21)

CHAPTER FOURTEEN

General Maxwell had been given a free hand to put down the Rebellion and this included authority to punish the participants.(*1*) But the way he went about this caused alarm in many quarters. Three of the leaders, P. H. Pearse, Thomas Mac-Donagh and Thomas J. Clarke, were shot on 3 May; four more including Pearse's brother Willie, on 4 May; another on 5 May; and three days later four more. Wimborne told Chalmers and Chalmers told the Prime Minister that Maxwell had frightened them by going on with the executions further than the Lord Lieutenant would have wished. 'Wimborne', said Chalmers, 'really knows nothing of what is going on and is jumpy as regards a responsibility which is not his.'(*2*) Asquith sent his private secretary, Bonham Carter, to French to say that he was a 'little surprised and perturbed by the drastic action of shooting so many rebel leaders'. He desired to be referred to before any sentence of death was passed on any woman; this referred particularly to the Countess Markievicz who was being tried for her spectacular part in the Rising.(*3*) Later, Asquith directed that Maxwell should be reminded that any wholesale punishment by death might easily cause a revulsion of feeling in Britain and lay up a store of future trouble in Ireland. French warned Maxwell in this sense, but added that there was no intention to interfere with his freedom of action or initiative.(*4*)

Nathan, on the evening before he left Dublin, went up to the Royal Hospital with Dillon who entered a very strong protest against the continuation of the execution of unknown men. Maxwell did not admit all his contentions, and Dillon gathered that he contemplated considerable further executions, but, with Nathan supporting Dillon's view, the General undertook to weigh the issues carefully and to look particularly at 'a list of A.O.H. men and other innocent men' Dillon had supplied. Redmond and others besides asked the Prime Minister to intervene; his military men had gone too far, they said, and had dragged out the executions intolerably. The total number executed was small, compared with the daily casualties in the war which ran into thousands, but to the Irish people it was, 'as though they watched a stream of blood coming from beneath a closed door'.(5) A message Asquith received on 8 May told of the general and bitter resentment in Ireland of the long drawn-out vengeance that was being executed on the insurgents and on comparatively little known insurgents too. The Irish Party sent him a resolution which said that – 'The continuance of military executions, carried out against persistent protests . . . has caused rapidly increasing bitterness amongst the large majority of the Irish people who had no sympathy with the insurrection', and asked that 'in the interests of the Empire, as well as of Ireland, no further executions should be allowed to take place . . . and martial law immediately withdrawn'. And on 11 May, Dillon made an extremely bitter speech in the House of Commons, moving the adjournment to demand an explanation of the Government's attitude towards further executions. The Prime Minister was being kept in the dark, he said, as to the secret shootings and imprisonments, and Dublin was being maddened by rumours of massacres. Redmond spoke also and renewed an appeal he had made a week earlier for a cessation of reprisals. The resignation of Birrell had deprived him of his one really dependable ally in the Government but his close relations with Birrell had never, he averred, given him any real power or authority. All his opinions had been overborne; all his suggestions rejected; while the Government had never given him any information bad or good about the state of the country.(6) Redmond had asked Asquith on 3 May to avoid wholesale executions for 'they would destroy our last hopes'. Asquith had told him that he had given orders to the War Office to go slowly, and he admitted that later he was shocked when he read the news of further shootings. Redmond begged him to promise that no one else would be executed, but Asquith said he could not give an absolute promise to that effect but, except in some very special case, that was his desire and intention. As for the rank and file, nothing would be done to them at all. As the shootings continued Redmond threatened to resign if any more executions took place; and he made a special plea for the life of Eoin MacNeill who, he said, had been a thorn in his flesh for years.

MacNeill, on observing that the Rising had run its course and, in an effort to prevent further conflict, wrote to Maxwell on 1 May asking for an interview and sent a copy of his letter to the Chief Secretary. Maxwell had him promptly arrested and court-martialled, and on 29 May he confirmed a sentence of penal servitude for life.(7) In the preliminary interrogation Major Price, the Army Intelligence Officer, gave a particularly good example of how little the Government knew of how the Rising had occurred and of the military's distrust of some of the Irish Party leaders by trying to induce MacNeill to involve Dillon and Devlin in the Rising!(8) It had been noted that Dillon was having his sons educated in a Benedictine school near Gorey run by a Father Sweetman which Abbot Marmion described to Redmond as 'a nest of Fenians and Sinn Féiners'.(9)

To neutralize the agitation for mercy a memorial was signed by 763 influential people in Dublin – Unionists all of them – protesting against any interference with the discretion of the Commander in Chief of the Forces in Ireland and the operation of martial law. Maxwell was not concerned with whether the Insurgents were comparatively known or not. He told Asquith on 9 May, in reply doubtless to an enquiry as to what he was doing, that he had confirmed no death sentence unless he was convinced by the evidence that the convict was either a leader of the movement or a commander of rebels engaged in shooting down His Majesty's troops or subjects. And, presumably, on that basis ninety-seven death sentences were commuted to penal servitude for various terms ranging from three years to life, and as things turned out, all these prisoners were released inside the next year or so. Asquith, meanwhile, as a result of all the pressure on him, had been concerning himself more actively with the situation, and secured an undertaking from Maxwell on 21 May that he would confirm no sentence of death without reference to him.(10) By that time some further executions had taken place but Maxwell had in fact informed the Prime Minister about them in advance. On 9 May he telegraphed the position regarding James Connolly and John McDermott who still remained to be tried. 'If convicted they must suffer the extreme penalty. They will be the last to suffer capital punishment, as far as I can now state'. They were in fact the last to be shot, but not the last of the 1916 men to suffer capital punishment. That distinction was reserved for Sir Roger Casement. Being key men in the Rising it would have been inconsistent with the other executions if the lives of Connolly and McDermott had been spared. Connolly, however, had been wounded in the G.P.O. and this raised a question that was put by the Prime Minister to Maxwell and dealt with by him in his reply, also of 9 May: 'Connolly having been reported fit to be tried, was tried to-day and sentenced to death. This I have confirmed. McDermott also tried, convicted, sentenced to death, confirmed. These will be shot at dawn of 11 May. In regard to Connolly's wound, he was shot above the ankle fracturing the bone but would recover in ordinary circumstances in three months'.

Maxwell took pains to explain his general policy. 'In view of the gravity of the Rebellion', he wrote, for the information of the Prime Minister, 'and its connection with German intrigue and propaganda and in view of the great loss of life and destruction of property resulting therefrom, the General Officer Commanding in Chief, Irish Command, has found it imperative to inflict the most severe sentences on the organizers of this detestable Rising and on the Commanders who took an actual part in the actual fighting which occurred. It is hoped that these examples will be sufficient to act as a deterrent to intriguers and to bring home to them that the murder of His Majesty's subjects or other acts calculated to imperil the safety of the realm will not be tolerated'. Asquith's intervention held up the execution of the two men but only for a day. On 11 May Kitchener wired Maxwell—'Unless you hear anything to the contary from Mr. Asquith you may carry out to-morrow the extreme sentence of death upon McDermott and Connolly'. Presumably he did not.

The case of Diarmuid Lynch, a member of the Supreme Council of the I.R.B., was particularly mentioned. On 20 May, by which date the court-martial verdict had not yet come up for confirmation, Maxwell told the Prime Minister that he was being bombarded about the execution of this man; but he wanted to reassure him that he would confirm no death sentence without consulting him. Lynch's life was spared.

Dillon was active all this time, making representations of one sort or another in individual cases, and these, and particularly his Parliamentary Questions, were methodically referred to Major Price for his observations. In connection with one of them – presumably an enquiry as to the nature of the evidence that P. H. Pearse had been in alliance with the Germans – Maxwell indicated that a letter written by Pearse on 1 May, when detained in Arbour Hill, was produced and proved at his trial containing the passage—'I understand that the German expedition on which I was counting actually set sail but was defeated by the British'. These words were the postscript to a letter to his mother which, with some poems he had also written, was withheld by Maxwell.(*11*) So far as we know neither the letter nor two of the poems was published before. Here, first of all, is the letter.

Arbour Hill Barracks,
Dublin.
1 May 1916.

My dear Mother,

You will I know have been longing to hear from me. I do not know how much you have heard since the last note I sent you from the G.P.O.

On Friday evening the Post Office was set on fire and we had to abandon it. We dashed into Moore Street and remained in the houses in Moore Street on Saturday evening. We then found that we were surrounded by troops and that we had practically no food.

We decided in order to prevent further slaughter of the civilian population and in the hope of saving the lives of our followers, to ask the General Commanding the British Forces to discuss terms. He replied that he would receive me only if I surrendered unconditionally and this I did.

I was taken to the Headquarters of the British Command in Ireland and there I wrote and signed an order to our men to lay down their arms.

All this I did in accordance with the decision of our Provisional Government who were with us in Moore Street. My own opinion was in favour of one more desperate sally before opening negotiations, but I yielded to the majority, and I think now the majority was right, as the sally would have resulted only in losing the lives of perhaps 50 or 100 of our men, and we should have had to surrender in the long run as we were without food.

I was brought in here on Saturday evening and later all the men with us in Moore Street were brought here. Those in the other parts of the City have, I understand, been taken to other barracks and prisons.

All here are safe and well. Willie and all the St Enda's boys are here. I have not seen them since Saturday, but I believe they are all well and that they are not now in any danger.

Our hope and belief is that the Government will spare the lives of all our followers, but we do not expect that they will spare the lives of the leaders. We are ready to die and we shall die cheerfully and proudly. Personally I do not hope or even desire to live, but I do hope and desire and believe that the lives of all our followers will be saved including the lives dear to you and me (my own excepted) and this will be a great consolation to me when dying.

You must not grieve for all this. We have preserved Ireland's honour and our own. Our deeds of last week are the most splendid in Ireland's history. People will say hard things of us now, but we shall be remembered by posterity and blessed by unborn generations. You too will be blessed because you were my mother.

If you feel you would like to see me, I think you will be allowed to visit me by applying to the Headquarters, Irish Command, near the Park. I shall I hope have another opportunity of writing to you.

Love to W.W.,* M.B.,† Miss Byrne, . . .‡ and your own dear self.

P.S.

I understand that the German expedition which I was counting on actually set sail but was defeated by the British.

That most moving document calls for two factual comments. First, the postscript, along with the summary of Pearse's court-

*'Wow-wow' (Margaret).
†Mary Bridget.
‡Miss Margaret Pearse suggests that illegible initials here may be those of a Cousin Margaret of whom Pearse was particularly fond.

martial speech which has been published before, indicates that he expected an expeditionary force as well as a shipment of arms. This was not part of the final arrangements with the Germans and one wonders how Pearse could have thought it was. Secondly, Pearse must have been told by the military that the letter would not be given to his mother, for on 3 May, as he waited for the firing-squad, he wrote another letter to her, also previously published, which withholds the description of the last day of the fighting in the G.P.O. area and the circumstances in which the decision was taken to surrender. This was duly delivered to Mrs Pearse with two of four poems that Pearse had managed to compose in those turbulent days. The two that are only now seeing the light of day were addressed to his mother and his brother Willie who had fought under him in the General Post Office. Here they are:

TO MY MOTHER

My gift to you hath been the gift of sorrow,
My one return for your rich gifts to me,
Your gift of life, your gift of love and pity,
Your gift of sanity, your gift of faith
(For who hath had such faith as yours
Since the old time, and what were my poor faith
Without your strong belief to found upon?)
For all these precious things my gift to you
Is sorrow. I have seen
Your dear face line, your face soft to my touch,
Familiar to my hands and to my lips
Since I was little:
I have seen
How you have battled with your tears for me,
And with a proud glad look, although your heart
Was breaking. O Mother (for you know me)
You must have known, when I was silent,
That some strange thing within me kept me dumb,
Some strange deep thing, when I should shout my love?
I have sobbed in secret
For that reserve which yet I could not master.
I would have brought royal gifts, and I have brought you
Sorrow and tears: and yet, it may be

That I have brought you something else beside—
The memory of my deed and of my name,
A splendid thing which shall not pass away.
When men speak of me, in praise or in dispraise,
You will not heed, but treasure your own memory
Of your first son.

P. H. Pearse.

Arbour Hill Detention Barracks,
1 May 1916.

TO MY BROTHER

O faithful!
Moulded in one womb,
We two have stood together all the years,
All the glad years and all the sorrowful years,
Own brothers : through good repute and ill,
In direst peril true to me,
Leaving all things for me, spending yourself
In the hard service that I taught to you,
Of all the men that I have known on earth,
You only have been my familiar friend,
Nor needed I another.

P. H. Pearse.

The Commander charged with the pacification of Ireland does not seem to have liked Pearse's surmise in the poem to his mother that she would be blessed in time because of him, and that the memory of his deed and name would live for ever. Why he should have suppressed the poem to his brother is not so clear, however. Some of the references in the letter make it clear that Pearse did not believe that Willie would be executed, nor would he, perhaps, had he not insisted at the court-martial that he had been immersed in the plans for the Rising from the beginning. The late Desmond Ryan told the author – and he had the story from eyewitnesses – that Willie Pearse practically condemned himself to death by the exultant attitude he adopted at the court-martial.

Dillon went to Asquith on behalf of Mrs Pearse and appears to have succeeded in extracting a promise from him that the bodies of the two brothers would be handed over to her for burial in consecrated ground. 'You know, I suppose', he said, 'the deep feeling which exists in Ireland on this matter. I may say that in my deliberate opinion this poor lady, Mrs Pearse, has been cruelly treated. She had but the two sons – and the second – Willie Pearse – with whom I had a slight personal acquaintance – was a most inoffensive creature and in no sense a leader amongst the rebels'.(*12*) But when Miss Margaret Pearse followed this up with a letter to Maxwell (25 May 1916), the G.O.C. telegraphed immediately to Asquith and induced him to change his mind. This would be a most undesirable concession, he said. It would have to be done in all cases if it was done in one. He had therefore refused Mrs Pearse. 'Irish sentimentality will turn these graves into martyrs' shrines to which annual processions, etc., will be made which will cause constant irritation in this country'. In any event 'the Prime Minister should know', he told Asquith's secretary, Bonham Carter, the next day 'that the bodies of all the executed rebels are buried in quicklime, without coffins, in the Arbour Hill Prison grounds. This I understand is the ordinary prison procedure. . . . Mr Dillon also presses that the papers, etc., found on Pearse or written by him should be delivered to the family. I enclose for the information of the Prime Minister copies of all we have; some of it is objectionable. I am sorry to refer such things but with all the Irish members on the warpath, I feel I ought to'.(*13*)

By this time Asquith had been to Ireland and back again in an effort to find a substitute for the system of governing Ireland that had manifestly failed. He announced that the Government was determined to find an agreed solution for the Irish problem and that Lloyd George had been put in charge of the negotiations. He put the Chief Secretaryship into temporary cold storage and sat for a day or two in Dublin Castle with Chalmers and Campbell, the Attorney General, looking at the problems of the office, particularly those which had been created by the executions and the large-scale imprisonments. On the whole, except for the Sheehy Skeffington case and some unexplained shootings of civilians in the North King Street area, there had been fewer bad blunders than one might have expected with the soldiery for a whole week in exclusive charge. As he moved about large crowds gathered to greet him. They 'cheered and were most civil, not a sign of any kind even of glumness. They are an extraordinary people. . . .' He had the same sort of reception in Belfast '—of all places. You never get to the bottom of this most perplexing and damnable country'.(*14*)

Up in the Viceregal Lodge where he stayed he unburdened himself to Campbell. Recent events had strengthened his conviction that the Lord Lieutenancy was a dangerous sham – the appearance without any reality of power – and an anachronism of a vicious kind. Any useful purposes which it still served would be much better obtained if the King came to reside in Ireland and travelled about the country for six weeks in the year. To his astonishment Campbell quite agreed. Asquith then said that the inference was that the Chief Secretaryship must be abolished, and a responsible Minister for Ireland appointed. But the problem was to get a man fit and acceptable for the job; Campbell suggested Walter Long but did not press it. Having discussed whether Carsonites and Redmondites could be got to agree on a general disarmament, Asquith also found Campbell very strongly of the opinion that now was the time to end the likelihood of a revival of the struggle of Ulster against Home Rule. Asquith wondered if an arrangement on the basis of the exclusion of Ulster could be introduced without delay, but Campbell doubted whether either Carson or Redmond, both of whose followings included a lot of irresponsibles and snipers, would or could venture on an agreement.(*15*)

Though he had shed responsibility for Irish affairs Nathan was deeply interested in these efforts and helped Sir Horace Plunkett to formulate a proposal to vest the powers of the Lord Lieutenant and the Chief Secretary in a small council of Irishmen appointed by the Crown which could include adequate representation for Ulster. But he was anxious that this immediate measure should not delay Asquith's attempt to reach agreement on the Home Rule question. The strange convulsion, as Plunkett called it, had predisposed the minds of politicians to settlement.(*16*) He was right. But Asquith's ideas for putting the Home Rule Act into operation in the middle of the war nearly broke up the Coalition – Lord Selbourne actually resigned – so the whole idea was dropped and Asquith returned to government through a Lord Lieutenant and Chief Secretary. Wimborne(*17*) was re-appointed as Lord Lieutenant and H. E. Duke became Chief Secretary. It was another slap in the face for the

Irish Party. They had disapproved of Asquith going to Ireland; it would be interpreted as an act of apology for General Maxwell's policy and it was to some extent so interpreted. He visited the prisoners in Richmond Barracks, found them 'very good-looking fellows with such lovely eyes' and ordered a drastic comb-out before they were transferred to England. But Dillon, too, had visited the prisoners – those in Stafford Jail – and one of them said that he 'gave us great praise for the great fight that we made'.(*18*)

While Asquith was in Ireland, Maxwell gave French the benefit of his far-seeing views on Irish nationalism. 'The political *raison d'être* of the movement does not differ so very materially from old other Home Rule movements. . . . The advanced Home Rulers became Sinn Féiners because they considered the Irish Home Rule Party under John Redmond was becoming too constitutional and self-seeking. They advocated and preached more revolutionary methods. It is thus very difficult to differentiate between Sinn Féiners and Redmondites. It is merely a question of degree. . . .

It appears to me that there is no doubt, though direct evidence is not easily procurable, that the Germans have through German Americans and revolutionary Clan na Gaels in America fomented the Sinn Féiners and the Citizen Army with vague promises and propaganda to rebellion. Had the enterprise of Sir Roger Casement succeeded the whole of the West of Ireland including Cork would have risen and I deliberately think that we have narrowly missed a most serious rebellion. . . . One danger must not be lost sight of . . . the younger generation is likely to be more revolutionary than their predecessors.

I think I can, however, assert that recent events have proved to the extremists that rebellion without ample arms and organization cannot succeed, and that they have no chance of success against trained soldiers'.(*19*)

Maxwell entered into a long defence of his position on 16 June 1916. Once more his forecasting was remarkably accurate. Efforts were being made, he declared, to discredit the military and to shift the blame for the outbreak on to the shoulders of the authorities. 'Censored correspondence of interned prisoners bear this out; for it shows a decided turn for the worse; whereas at first their letters were humble and apologetic, now the tone has become defiant, and shows that they think themselves national heroes.

That there is a strong recrudescence of Sinn Féinism is true; young priests and innocent women . . . encourage this in every possible way. Though the rebellion was condemned it is now being used as a lever to bring on Home Rule, or an Irish Republic.

There is a growing feeling that out of Rebellion more has been got than by constitutional methods, hence Mr Redmond's power is on the wane, therefore this desire to curry favour with the people on the part of the M.Ps. by agitating for the release of Sinn Féiners.

It is becoming increasingly difficult to differentiate between a Nationalist and a Sinn Féiner.

Mourning badges, Sinn Féin flags, demonstrations at Requiem Masses, the resolutions of public bodies are all signs of the growth of Sinn Féin.

Recruiting in Ireland has practically ceased.

The influence which keeps Ulster and the North quiet is the knowledge that they can have their arms and can, if need be, defend themselves. They will never consent to disarm or to allow more men to leave as recruits for the Army as long as the feeling is what it is.

The bulk of brains and money is in the North. Home Rule in Ireland without these is impossible and the Nationalists know this; the North being mainly industrial denies the possibility of being governed by people of the South, who are mainly agricultural or publicans or vice versa.

Scattered over the South are a large number who are in entire sympathy with the North and view with the greatest apprehension being left to the mercy of a Home Rule Nationalist Government; in contrast, there are a number of Nationalists in the North who do not wish to be excluded from the Home Rule Government. . . . If there was a General Election very few, if any, of existing Nationalist M.Ps. would be re-elected so there is a danger that Mr Redmond's party would be replaced by others perhaps less amenable to reason'.(20)

CHAPTER FIFTEEN

Asquith had a précis prepared for him of the events leading up to the Rising and French sent the Army Council at their request a report on the inadequacy of the steps taken by the G.O.C. Ireland (Friend) to anticipate it. Neither of these documents is dated but they were both probably written before the end of the first week in May 1916. Asquith underlined the passage in the précis that quoted Nathan's declaration to the Adjutant General on 10 April that he did not believe that the Sinn Féin leaders meant insurrection or that the Volunteers had sufficient arms if the leaders did mean it. It was these words that may have finished Nathan. In point of time, they were later than the latest statement of Birrell's and, as we saw, they prevented the military from taking the action that they considered necessary. But this does not mean that Birrell would have disagreed with Nathan's appraisal of the position, or that his overall responsibility was in any way lessened thereby.

Asquith had learned from the précis that on 22 March, the Director of Military Intelligence (D.M.I.), Major General G. M. W. MacDonagh, who was a member of the Supreme General Staff and whom Winston Churchill regarded as the best Intelligence Officer in Europe,(*1*) had informed French that he had received information from 'an absolutely reliable source' that a Rising in Ireland was contemplated at an early date, and that the Irish extremists were in communication with Germany with a view to obtaining German assistance. The Rising was timed to take place on 22 April and the extremists had asked Germany to supply arms and ammunition to Limerick by that date. Acting on similar information, it was said that Admiral Sir Lewis Bayly at Queenstown had issued a stringent order for patrolling the Irish coast.

Asquith observed that French had held a conference with the

Irish Government Authorities on 23 March, the day following the D.M.I.'s. communication, and he pertinently enquired who was at the conference and whether the communication had been read at it, or referred to. We do not know what answers were given to these questions but we do know independently that Birrell and Wimborne and Friend were present at the meeting, but that the communication was not before the meeting. In considering this matter a letter of 28 April from Brade, the Secretary of the Army Council, to French is important. Even before the Rising was suppressed, the Council were concerned with disciplinary issues. They had been informed that on the day the disturbances commenced Friend was in England, and that certain officers attended a race meeting at a distance from their stations and were reported to have been taken by the Insurgents and held as hostages. 'On 22 March 1916,' Brade went on, 'a secret memo. on the state of Ireland was sent from the War Office to your Irish staff, *and ... was communicated to Friend*.* There is further reason to believe that on 16 April Friend received information from the General Officer Commanding Queenstown (Stafford) ... that two submarines and a vessel containing arms had left Germany for Ireland. In connection with these two events ... it is noted that Sir Roger Casement was arrested on 20 April and the vessel sunk on 21 April.' French was asked to report fully the circumstances under which, in view of the very serious warnings that had presumably been received by him, Friend was not present in his command, and the officers were allowed to absent themselves from their stations.

French incorporated his reply to Brade's questions in a general report for the Army Council on the adequacy of the steps taken by Friend to forestall the Rising, but he did not deny the statement that the secret memorandum – otherwise the D.M.I.'s. communication – had been communicated to Friend, so we must assume that it was, and we know that Friend had received the letter of 16 April from Brigadier General Stafford and had handed it to Nathan on the 17th. Looking at the phrasing of Brade's statement – 'a secret memo. on the state of Ireland was sent from the War Office to your Irish staff, and ... was communicated to Friend' – it seems as if the memorandum was sent by the D.M.I. direct to Major Price and that Price showed it to

*Author's italics.

136

Friend. This interpretation is supported by the fact that French, in writing to the Army Council stressed that Irish Intelligence was really, but anomalously, a matter for the War Office and not for him, before going on to praise the arrangements Friend had made to anticipate an outbreak 'although he did not apparently think that there was likely to be an overt act of rebellion'. There was nothing at all to show, he said, that Friend was unprepared for a rising so far as the disposition of his troops was concerned, and when the emergency arose it was dealt with energetically and successfully in accordance with his pre-arranged plan. As regards his absence in London on Easter Monday he gave the plausible enough explanation that the real danger had passed with the capture of Casement and the arms ship, and MacNeill's call-off of the manoeuvres announced for Easter Sunday. Birrell, Nathan and Wimborne – as distinct from the military – may never have seen the secret document with its full month's warning of a rising with German aid. If they knew about it, they certainly did not treat its contents seriously. Birrell and Nathan might have so acted in any event, because the warning did not square with their own preconceptions. The projected landings on the south-west coast of Ireland came as news to Nathan when he was given Brigadier General Stafford's letter on the Monday of Holy Week, and by that time he had arranged to bring his sister-in-law and her children to Dublin for Easter and had invited Birrell and Dorothy Stopford to join them; and, as we saw, Birrell would have come were it not for the Cabinet crisis. Nathan's arrangements for a house party would not have been made had he expected a rising, and some of his guests had arrived by the time he saw Stafford's letter. And it must be said that those who did see the secret memorandum – French, Friend and Price – were not impressed by it sufficiently to make it a cause for a show-down with the Civil Government, whose advice they had consistently followed. No special action was taken either on foot of Brigadier General Stafford's message which was based on what he had learned from Admiral Bayly at Queenstown. Nathan and the Inspector General of the R.I.C. were both 'doubtful whether there was any foundation for the *rumour*'*(2) and Stafford, himself, did not appear to be unduly worried. There had been alarms before and nothing had come of them.

*Author's italics.

What was 'the absolutely reliable source' of the D.M.I's. information? One cannot be positive about this either but it would appear to have been revealed in the White Paper containing documents relative to the Sinn Féin movement(3) published by the British Government in 1921, particularly when this White Paper is read in conjunction with Admiral Sir William James's book *The Eyes of the Navy, 40 O.B. or How the War Was Won* by H. C. Hoy, and *Strange Intelligence* by H. C. Bywater and H. C. Ferraby. The source was almost certainly the radio messages that were intercepted by the British Navy as they passed between the German Embassy in Washington and the Foreign Office in Berlin and deciphered in Room 40 of the Admiralty under the direction of Captain (later Sir Reginald) Hall. This interception had been taking place practically from the outbreak of the War and, so far as Ireland was concerned, the first advantage it conferred on the British was to add to their knowledge of Casement's movements towards the end of 1914.

According to Hall's confidential secretary, H. C. Hoy, the listening stations on the east coast of England intercepted as many as 2,000 German fleet signals and wireless communications a day. These were all, of course, transmitted in codes which were frequently changed but not one of the messages ever completely defeated Hall's experts. The unparalleled importance of Room 40 O.B. was first recognized, Hoy says, when, twenty-four hours before the Dogger Bank action, the British knew the number of German ships that had left for the scene and the exact time of their departure; and it owed its ability to continue its work undiscovered to a Frenchman who threw the Germans off the scent by making them believe that some highly-placed person in Berlin was giving away their secrets. One of the tit-bits the British gave the Frenchman to maintain this belief was the news of the departure of Casement from Berlin 'in order to lead the Irish Rebellion'. The secret of the intended Irish Rebellion was out, he told the Germans, and Paris was in possession of the course of Casement's journey and the number of the U-boat that conveyed him.(4)

In the particular sequence of messages intercepted between 10 February and 21 March 1916, the agreement for collaboration between the revolutionary group in Ireland, working through the Clan na Gael leader, John Devoy, in New York, and the

German Government was uncovered. This radio correspondence continued right up to the Rising, but by 21 March the intention to rise, the date of the Rising, the nature of the German contribution and the place of landing were firmly known to the British, although there were variations later in points of detail. The D.M.I's. 'secret memo.' of 22 March had said that the Rising was fixed to take place on 22 April – which was Easter Saturday – and that the Germans had been asked to supply arms and ammunition to Limerick by that date. Easter Saturday was the date announced to the Germans by John Devoy in mid-February and the telegram in which he did so specified Limerick as the place of landing.

What adds an element of mystery to the story, however, is that the subsequent variations in place and date of landing were not the subject of subsequent 'secret memoranda'. The message from Stafford that Friend handed to Nathan on 17 April was out of date in that it spoke of a contemplated landing on the south-west coast, not specifically Tralee Bay, and of a Rising fixed for Easter Saturday, the 22nd, although this date was changed later. This may mean that the interception was not as complete as it was claimed to be. But intercepting on a vast scale was taking place, and it is easy to understand that Admiral Hall was most careful that the means he was employing should not become known. He would have preferred that the rebellion in Ireland should succeed rather than that Britain should lose what his biographer described as 'our most valuable weapon against Germany'.(5)

But talk of 'an absolutely reliable source' seems to have carried no conviction in military circles; Friend looked at his precautionary arrangements, as he had done in the case of earlier warnings, but did no more. And so far as the Civil Government was concerned the effect of the interception was stultified by the failure of the Admiralty to make any direct communication to them. Whatever trickled through to them via Bayly, Stafford and Friend made little or no impact. Bayly was a very discreet officer and appears to have given his opposite military number at Queenstown nothing more than the merest hint of what he knew to be afoot. In any event the manner in which the item reached Dublin Castle left the Executive with five days' warning instead of a month's. But we must repeat that the Executive would have been unlikely to pay any more attention to the information had they heard of it directly and earlier; the only thing that would have moved them to more robust action would have been an indication of the 'absolutely reliable source', and that was out of the question. Even the Cabinet were not given that. It was not given to Birrell at any rate.

Bayly played a vital part in scotching the plans for the Rising. Believing as he did in 'the wonderful correctness of the Admiralty intelligence' he organized a close look-out for a disguised German arms ship. He sent trawlers to watch the coast between the Aran Islands and the Kenmare River, including the Shannon, Tralee Bay, and Dingle Bay. The light cruiser *Gloucester* and four destroyers, sent as reinforcements from the Grand Fleet, as well as a few sloops joined in the search. No one knew where the arms ship would be met with, but when news was sent to Queenstown of a concentration of cars near Fenit, in Tralee Bay, a much disaffected district, a look-out was kept for her in that neighbourhood. One day Loop Head signal station, at the mouth of the Shannon, reported a steamer, the *Aud,* acting in a suspicious manner. Two trawlers followed her, and Bayly sent H.M.S. *Zinnia* and H.M.S. *Bluebell* which were in the vicinity. The *Zinnia* closed with the steamer and, on finding nothing suspicious, was about to let her resume her journey when they received a wireless message from Bayly to escort her into Queenstown and, if she resisted, to sink her. Next morning Bayly and his niece were on the veranda of Admiralty House, Queenstown, when the *Aud* with its escort of naval vessels arrived off Daunt's Rock and were witnesses to an explosion which sent the German steamer to the bottom of the channel. A diver later recovered some rifles which bore evidence that they had been manufactured in Orleans in 1902 and captured by the Germans in the Russian retreat at the beginning of the war.

On 20 April, Admiral Sir H. B. Jackson, the First Sea Lord, congratulated Bayly on his success which 'probably saved a much more serious outbreak in the west, and was well carried out in every way. If', he added significantly, 'the other Government departments had taken our *hints*;* I daresay the whole thing would have been stopped in the bud, but even Casement's capture did not seem to move them.'(6)

*Author's italics.

The interception of messages between the U.S.A. and Germany was not the only source of enemy information the British had; their postal censorship yielded its quota of results; and they had agents well placed who kept them informed of enemy movements. Hoy says that it was by this means it was learned that Casement was going to Germany in October 1914. They flashed the news to the Atlantic Fleet and Casement's liner was boarded, but the officer who conducted the search failed to identify the Irishman. He had shaved off his beard, washed his face with buttermilk to get a fair complexion, and thrown his papers overboard. The British received a certain amount of help also from the Americans; the F.B.I. in a raid on the German office in New York on 18 April 1916, had found a transcript of a message from Dublin asking that the arms should not be landed before the night of Sunday, 23 April. This message never reached the *Aud*, however, which was already at sea and had no wireless. This particular piece of news came too late to be of any use to the British, but if the earlier information from the 'absolutely reliable source' had been properly transmitted and its importance emphasized and accepted, it is difficult not to believe that the Rising would have been prevented. In fact the misuse of this information threw the Irish Executive back on their own domestic intelligence service which was not of a high order. The information it supplied was usually too general in character, and when it was specific, it related to relatively unimportant points. There was no penetration to the heart of the conspiracy and little evidence of ability to make use of what was learned. Up to the middle of Holy Week, the intention to rise was only known to a few people, and the Government had no 'friends' among them. Nathan gave particulars to the Royal Commission of 'reports' that were received in March and April; but these, with one exception, were from people who without difficulty could have belonged to the rank and file of the Volunteers but would have got no further. In drafting his statement for the Commission Nathan described these persons as Dublin informers but, at the suggestion of Birrell's secretary, Magill, who was a Dublin man, the references to informers was struck out and a neutral word substituted. 'The word informer', Magill told Nathan, 'sounds so badly in an Irish ear that there is sure to be a howl about it. I always remember an old ballad which, referring to such an informer, breaks out—"May the hearthstone of Hell be his rest bed forever".'

Nathan told the Commission that until the *Aud* and the submarine put in an appearance on the Kerry coast, the Executive had no definite proof of any connection between what he termed the anti-British party in Ireland and the foreign enemy. It was, of course, known, he said, that Clan na Gael was in alliance with the German organizations in America, but this statement reveals how little he really knew about a situation of which Admiral Hall was so well informed. The veneer of contact with the German-American organizations had given way since 1914 to a close working arrangement between Devoy and the German Embassy in Washington whose staff in fact regarded the old Fenian as an agent of theirs. For decades Devoy had been a worry to the Castle authorities. At home, they thought of Clarke and Daly, and latterly of Casement and MacNeill at the apex of the Volunteer organization, but in fact they did not know who their real adversaries were. This was the crucial point at which the Castle's domestic Intelligence service failed.

The Director of Military Intelligence in his reference to absolutely reliable information had mentioned Irish extremists as being in league with the Germans. These were the Military Committee of the I.R.B. or, as they were more usually called, the Military Council, and they were properly described as extremists though the word hurts some susceptibilities. The Council had come into being in June 1915 or thereabouts, but as early as August 1914, shortly after the outbreak of the war, a special committee of the Clan na Gael met Count von Bernstorff, the German Ambassador to the United States, in New York, and informed him of their intention to organize an armed revolt in Ireland and asked for military assistance.(7) This decision was communicated to the Supreme Council of the I.R.B. in Ireland who agreed that a rebellion, with or without German aid, should take place before the war ended.(8) The constitution of the I.R.B. did not provide for a military committee although the appointment of committees for special purposes was a normal practice, and one would have thought that the setting-up of a group to plan the Rising would have required a very special decision on the part of the Supreme Council and continuous control by that body thereafter. This was not the case, nor was the Military Council appointed by the Supreme Council but by the Officer Board or Executive which at that time comprised the President, Denis McCullough; the Treasurer, T. J. Clarke; and Diarmuid Lynch, who was acting as secretary in the place of John McDermott, then in prison. The President, who resided in Belfast, was apparently not present on the occasion, and it fell to the lot of the acting Secretary to nominate the Council. This was to consist of P. H. Pearse, Joseph Plunkett and Eamonn Ceannt, who were high ranking officers in the Irish Volunteers.(9) Later, Clarke and McDermott 'actively co-operated'.(10)

The Military Council appears to have been a device for formalizing preparations already begun. Plunkett had gone to Germany early in 1915 and made an arrangement with Von Bethmann Holweig at the Foreign Office to send a cargo of arms and ammunition to Ireland at a date in the spring of the following year when it was hoped that a Rising and a German offensive on the Western front would prove complementary embarrassments to the British.(11) But although its existence was later made known to the Supreme Council of the I.R.B. the Military Council does not appear to have made any reports to that body, notwithstanding a provision in the Constitution for the subordination of the military arm to the civil. Secrecy was undoubtedly indispensable if surprise was to be achieved, but it was pushed to such extremes that it ultimately defeated its purpose. With a few exceptions the key figures in the Volunteer movement were only alerted in Holy Week, and their instructions were so rigid that they were left with no possibility of improvising when, as in Kerry, the basic plan went wrong. The secret was well-kept, so well-kept in fact that the wide-awake Bulmer Hobson, himself a former member of the Supreme Council, who was meeting the members of the Military Council daily in connection with the work of the Volunteers, only tumbled to the existence of this enclave within the I.R.B. and what they were up to a few days before the Rising took place.

The Military Council consisted of Irish Volunteer Officers only until January 1916 but in that month James Connolly had to be made a member of it to prevent him from leading the Citizen Army into a precipitate rising on their own account. In his *Workers' Republic* he had been calling for action with ever greater vehemence. The Kingdom of Heaven could only be taken by violence, he declared on Christmas Day 1915 and a few weeks later he insisted that the time for Ireland's battle was *now* (22 January 1916). He had been unaware of the existence of the Military Council and doubted whether the Volunteers had any serious intentions. His mind on both scores was changed for him by the I.R.B. as the result of close discussions in a secret rendezvous.(*12*) And Thomas MacDonagh, who was the last man to be invited to join the Military Council – this was in early April 1916 – was also probably until that time ignorant of its existence, although he was the friend, teaching colleague and close associate of Pearse. His adherence brought the membership of the Committee up to seven and all seven signed the Proclamation of the Republic and paid for doing so with their lives.

They had hoped at one time to win Eoin MacNeill over to their way of thinking and to get him to sign the Proclamation, but this they failed to achieve. The I.R.B. had encouraged MacNeill in the formation of the Irish Volunteers, but MacNeill never became an I.R.B. man nor, indeed, a Republican. He was a man of known patriotic but moderate political views; his orthodox Catholicism,* apart from anything else, made secret societies repugnant to him, and he was chary of having anything to do with the Germans. On these latter two points the Proclamation of the Republic was explicit : Ireland's manhood had been organized and trained primarily through the secret revolutionary organization, the Irish Republican Brotherhood, and was seizing an opportunity to strike, supported by 'gallant allies in Europe'. MacNeill was opposed to direct offensive action not merely on religious grounds but because he was only too well aware that in numbers, equipment and training the Volunteers were not fitted to challenge the occupation forces in the field. He believed in remaining in a defensive position, of preserving the Volunteer organization and its arms intact, and to be ready at the end of the war to insist on England's promises of self-government being fulfilled. He was also ready to commit the Volunteers if the imposition of conscription was attempted or if an effort was made by the Government to disarm them and suppress their organization. In that event they would rely on guerrilla

*As late as 1937 a distinguished theologian held that the Irish revolt was not legitimate, even though the sympathies of Catholics and free men were with Ireland.(*13*)

tactics rather than stake all on the seizure of Dublin and other key points.(*14*) In so far as there was an official policy of the Irish Volunteers, this was it, and it was this that the I.R.B. through the Military Council, set out to undermine.

They were well placed to do it. They were exactly half of the Headquarters Staff of the Volunteers. Pearse was the Director of Organization, Plunkett the Director of Military Operations, MacDonagh the Director of Training and Ceannt the Director of Communications. The other four posts were held by Mac-Neill, who was the Chief of Staff; Bulmer Hobson, Quarter-master General; J. J. O'Connell, the Chief of Inspection; and John Fitzgibbon, the Director of Recruiting. One member of this quartette, Hobson, although an I.R.B. man, was a strong adherent of the official defence policy. Having scented the existence of the revolutionary group within the Volunteer Executive he spoke to MacNeill who was reluctant, at first, to believe what he was told. He had been concerned at Connolly's insistence that he would take out the Irish Citizen Army, alone if necessary, if the others would not join him. This threat was a greater embarrassment to the I.R.B. who had laid their own long-term plans, and, through Pearse, they got MacNeill to speak to Connolly. MacNeill failed, however, to dissuade him, even by saying that he was mistaken if he thought that the Volunteers would fight rather than see the Citizen Army destroyed. MacNeill must have come away from the conversation feeling anything but happy, but Pearse later assured him that he had been more successful and had won Connolly around to his way of thinking. This was a *double entendre*: Connolly had joined the I.R.B.; Pearse and his I.R.B. associates had established an accord with the Labour leader; between them they had concocted a plan of action. The time for action had already been settled with the Germans.

The plan envisaged a general mobilization of the Volunteers throughout the whole of Ireland, the seizure of strategic points in Dublin city, the declaration there of the Irish Republic with a Provisional Government, and action in the neighbourhood of the Curragh and Athlone to forestall the expected pressure from these British encampments on the Volunteers in the centre of the capital. The Cork Volunteers were to work simultaneously towards Macroom and link up with the Kerry Brigade which, in turn, was to connect with the Volunteers in Clare, Limerick and Galway. To all these men from Cork to Galway who were recognized to be badly equipped, the arms and ammunition to be landed at Fenit by the Germans were to be distributed. Volunteers from Ulster were to occupy positions from the Shannon towards the South.(*15*) It was hoped that the Germans would support the outbreak by a diversion on the East coast of England, by Zeppelin raids along the South-East, and by sending a submarine into Dublin Bay that could deal with British reinforcements coming in by sea. Perhaps, too, they might send some German officers to lend their experience in the fight.

MacNeill's uneasiness revived a little later, as Pearse's attitude to the use of physical force became apparent. He prepared a letter which was read at a meeting of the Volunteer Executive in February 1916, in which he expressed his belief that military action without the prospect of success, and the action itself as distinct from some future advantage that might result from non-success, was morally wrong, while killing in the course of such action would be murder. Calculation of the possibilities, he insisted, should not be made to depend on so-called feelings or premonitions or on the adoption of *a priori* maxims. No man was entitled to impose his feelings or his unreasoned propensities in a matter involving the fate of his country and fellow countrymen. A number of these had been expounded which MacNeill found untenable such as that Ireland must take military action during the War, that Ireland had always struck too late, and that they should now take the initiative.

MacNeill's letter was not discussed nor was any action taken on it. The situation was allowed to drift. MacNeill's position was understood but the inner I.R.B. group had no intention of following suit. They hoped for success with German aid; but without success they believed that the spilling of their blood was a necessary sacrifice. They had accepted the notion that the Irish people had become degraded and required to be redeemed by a feat of arms. Pearse, who might have spoken for them all, was prepared to admit that MacNeill's arguments were right, logical and reasonable, but he preferred to follow his own sense of what the situation demanded.

The secrecy imposed on them by the plans to which they were committed led these men into a number of actions which they justified to themselves on the grounds of military necessity. All of these were aimed at their colleagues in the Volunteer Executive. Pearse, availing of his position as Director of Organization, and others conveyed secretly to the principal Volunteer officers in the country, many of whom had previously been sworn into the I.R.B., instructions for military dispositions to be taken up. Most of these men were unaware of the division of opinion within the Executive, and it was from some of them that Mac-Neill and company learned by the merest accident what was afoot. This led to a protest by MacNeill to the Volunteer Executive and to a decision which was generally accepted that no special orders should in future be issued to the organization without his signature.(16) On learning later that instructions had been given to destroy bridges in a certain eventuality, MacNeill raised the subject of an insurrection afresh with MacDonagh, as they walked home together one day from University College, only to be reproved for not believing the assurances he had already been given. In the course of Holy Week the document Alderman Kelly read to the Corporation and which it was sought to father on the Government, was concocted – probably by Joseph Plunkett who is said to have revelled in all sorts of stratagems. This was not directed against the Government but was intended to fool MacNeill and to provide justification for the initiative the Military Council had made ready to take. It did in fact deceive MacNeill at first, so much so that following a meeting of the Volunteer Executive on Spy Wednesday night he issued an Order warning the Volunteers to be on guard against the Government's plan to suppress them. Next evening, however, Hobson and O'Connell overheard a conversation which revealed to them that the Rising had been fixed for Easter Sunday, and they hurried out to Dundrum to tell MacNeill. Though it was after midnight, MacNeill took his lieutenants straight off with him to St Enda's College, got Pearse out of bed, and in a towering rage told him what he thought of the fraud that had been practised on him and the way his authority had been flouted. Pearse admitted that a Rising had been intended for the Sunday, and would not listen to any suggestion that it should be put off, to which MacNeill answered that he would do everything he could to stop it, short of ringing up Dublin Castle. He left Pearse then to his contemplation, and later drafted an Order giving Hobson and O'Connell command over the Volunteers in Dublin and the country and cancelling all previous Orders issued by Pearse 'or by any other person heretofore'.

Early next morning while MacNeill was still in bed, Mac-Donagh and McDermott came out and tried to get him to change his mind. They held a winning card when they told him that an arms ship was on its way from Germany. MacNeill saw that this changed the situation; either the initiative which this presented to the Volunteers had to be taken or the British would undoubtedly move against them. But this was Good Friday, the day on which the hopes of the Military Council slumped disastrously. Casement and Bailey were taken prisoners that day, so were Collins and Stack; the *Aud* was captured and led away towards Cork harbour and self-destruction, and the men who were sent from Dublin to help Stack in his part of the enterprise had been accidentally drowned. The 'extremists' were now completely on their own, although they did not know this until the afternoon of Easter Saturday because of Major Price's astute move in warning the newspapers to keep the Kerry happenings out of that morning's editions. The fight they had planned, if it was to take place at all, would have to be fought without the German consignment of rifles, machine guns and ammunition. Casement and his companions had come ashore on Banna Strand in circumstances that confirmed Casement in his determination to warn MacNeill and the Volunteers against embarking on a rising. And Monteith succeeded, after the arrest of Casement and Bailey, in sending the warning to Dublin; but though he addressed it to MacNeill, it was delivered to Connolly in Liberty Hall.

On Good Friday afternoon the revolutionary group arrested Hobson intending to hold him prisoner until he could no longer hinder their plans. Hobson managed, however, to inform MacNeill of what had happened and urged him to do all he could to send out the recall instructions on which Hobson himself had been working. MacNeill acted with determination. He got a group of officers together and despatched them all over the country with a note which declared that the Volunteers had been completely deceived. (There was an obvious ambiguity here: who had deceived them? MacNeill meant the Military Council element within the Volunteer Executive but he forbore from condemning them publicly.) All orders for special action were thereby cancelled – his message said – and on no account was action to be taken. He followed this up with the countermanding notice in the *Sunday Independent* which had to be drafted with greater care – because MacNeill did not want to help the Government to any understanding of what had gone on behind the scenes. It referred to the 'very critical position', which might have been an allusion to any or all of the things that had happened in recent days, and rescinded all orders for parades, marches or *other movements** of Irish Volunteers. Hindsight enables us to see the significance of the reference to other movements. This notice, as we saw, had an effect that was not intended. It ensured its object, that the Rising that was planned for four o'clock on Easter Sunday afternoon did not take place, but it led MacNeill and the Government alike into believing that that was the end of the affair, whereas the Military Council decided to go ahead at midday on the following day, Easter Monday, despite everything that had happened, and sent out their own officers in an endeavour to undo the effects of Mac-Neill's counteraction. In order, however, to cloak the decision to rise on the Monday, they confirmed MacNeill's cancellation of the Easter Sunday manoeuvres, and Pearse told MacNeill in a note that this had been done because, as he said, the leading men would not have obeyed MacNeill's countermand without his, Pearse's confirmation. MacNeill, therefore, more than anybody else was overwhelmed when he learned on Easter Monday that the Rising had begun.

However, of all the division in the Volunteer Executive, of all the moves and countermoves, the Government knew absolutely nothing and this is all the more extraordinary because so many people, including some on the fringe of things, knew that a revolt was due to take place that Easter week-end. The British Intelligence system in Ireland had failed hopelessly. But Intelligence had been defective on the Irish side too. It would have been the easiest thing in the world to take Dublin Castle had the revolutionaries gone to the trouble to find out, which they could have done quite easily, that it was held by a mere handful of soldiers. The capture of the Castle, the stronghold of British rule for centuries, would have added enormously to the prestige of the

*Author's italics.

149

Rising, without affecting the outcome of it. But it was apparently not part of their plan to seize the Castle, because it would require too large a force to hold it.(*17*)

As Nathan conferred at the Viceregal Lodge, the Military Council of the I.R.B. conferred in the town. Nathan decided on action after Monday; the others decided to act on Monday. Nathan, therefore, in racing parlance, was pipped at the post. Both sides had been considering the likely action of the other. It is certain that Nathan did not anticipate a rising on the Monday – all the portents were against this. He could understand resistance to a disarming of the Volunteers and to the arrest of the leaders and his postponement of this step for a few days was to ensure that this would be done properly. Anything else seemed irrational to him. He did not know, however, the calibre of the men he was dealing with. They were men committed to action, and committed to each other, and they were now in the dilemma that, despite the odds, they had to fight or be arrested, see their followers disarmed and the physical force movement fizzle out in futility. Instead of waiting for the Castle to act against them, they took the initiative, putting into action on the Monday the plan for Sunday that had been thwarted by MacNeill's intervention. But they were unable of course to regain the momentum of the Sunday. Confusion was widespread. There had been time since the cancellation in the Sunday morning newspaper for consideration of the position, and some men could see the division that existed at the top. MacNeill's phrase 'Volunteers completely deceived' had suggested this and had alerted some of them to the possibility that bad leadership would involve them in a disaster comparable to those that destroyed the freedom movements of earlier times. In the upshot the Rising was largely confined to Dublin but even in Dublin, only 1,600 men, including some 200 of Connolly's Citizen Army, mobilized instead of possibly three or four times that number, and with this force little more could be done than to occupy a few strategically placed buildings. The original idea of holding a continuous line forming a loop through the centre of the city had to be abandoned and no alternative plan existed to meet the altered circumstances.(*18*) There was no time now for revision, for the production of a plan for Dublin only, because, of course, the justification of a rising in the South and West disappeared with the sinking of the *Aud*. And the Government had no difficulty in isolating the occupied city areas, and treating them, in Nathan's phrase, as a series of Sydney Street affairs. No wonder that Connolly said 'we're going out to be slaughtered'.(*19*)

Nathan pondered over the problem as he read the newspapers after the Rising and prepared his case for the Royal Commission. What could have been done had they believed it was going to break out on the Easter Monday morning? 'I suppose strong guards at all public buildings – at least a dozen of them – would have prevented the few that did fall into the Volunteers' hands from meeting that fate but this would not have made the insurrection much less formidable than it was. An average of five men in each of say 400 private buildings is a proposition requiring a very big force on a very long line to tackle or the demolition of the buildings. I hope some effort is being made by the military authorities to discover exactly what were the places and orders for the insurrection and that they have not disposed of all of the prisoners who could give information as to this'.(*20*)

Nathan would have had this information had the police succeeded in placing an agent inside the Military Council of the I.R.B. But the police, of course, were unaware that such a body existed, a body that was able to start a rising on its own with the minimum of reference to its own superiors, and in the teeth of opposition from the President of the Irish Volunteers, a body that was able to encompass men in it who turned out on the instructions of their officers without understanding on whose behalf the officers were acting. It seems incontestable, as Mac-Neill said at his own court-martial afterwards, that 'no authorized body of the Irish Volunteers ever gave authorization for that insurrection'. It was produced, in effect, by a *coup d'état,* and in unavoidable circumstances of secrecy that were as much its undoing as anything else.

MacNeill at his court-martial said that on Easter Sunday afternoon about five o'clock his efforts to prevent the Rising had succeeded. On Monday morning about eleven o'clock they had been undone and he had come to the conclusion that something had happened in the meantime which had caused those whom he had overborne the day before to go back on their undertaking. He believed they had come to the conclusion that their action was inevitable, having probably heard of the decision taken at the meeting in the Viceregal Lodge to arrest the entire body of the Irish Volunteers, including MacNeill himself. This, he believed, was the cause of the insurrection. 'I have no doubt of it', he added. 'Nothing else could explain it. The men who told me that I had compelled them to act as I wished them to act – those men I knew them well and I will answer for them. They were men of honour. They were truthful and honourable men. They gave that assurance on the evening of Easter Sunday and I had no reason to doubt it.'(21) But they had not *heard* of the Viceregal Lodge decision; they had just assumed it.

CHAPTER SIXTEEN

Nathan was the first witness to appear before the Royal Commission when it held its first session in London on 18 May under the chairmanship of Lord Hardinge of Penshurst. He based his evidence on an elaborate statement he had prepared from official records in which he described the movement that led up to the Rising, the steps they had taken to deal with it and the warnings they had received immediately before the outbreak. All of this with numerous supporting appendices he submitted; while for his own use, he made ready a mass of other material which included lists, broken down into different categories, of persons who were likely to have helped the enemy in the event of a landing. One of these was Edward de Valera whose services at Blackrock College, it was alleged, had been dispensed with earlier because of his extreme pro-German and Sinn Féin views. Among the material Nathan made available to the Commission was a list of 'disaffected clergymen', otherwise Catholic priests who were involved in the Irish Volunteer movement but this he thought it would be inadvisable to publish. He also made ready particulars of Volunteer finances, supplied to him by Major Price, with extracts from a Bank account operated jointly by Eoin MacNeill and by the O'Rahilly who had been killed in the fighting. Among reports from various persons on disaffection that he handed in to the Commission was an interesting one from Canon James Hannay better known as the novelist George A. Birmingham (29 November 1915) in which he referred to the Sinn Féin movement as 'I knew it at its inception when I was myself greatly affected by it and when I gave some help to its propaganda'.

Nathan believed that the I.R.B. and the Volunteer Executive – both of them together – must have contemplated the Insurrection for 19 April; but, as we know, the Volunteer Executive as such had nothing to do with it. The I.R.B. as early as 1914 had decided in principle in favour of a rising before the end of the war, but the plans were laid, a decision taken and a date fixed about April 1915, by the Military Council. Pearse, at that time, correctly anticipating that a rising would end badly for him – he wrote a poem about the road before him and the death he would meet at the end of it – set about arranging his personal affairs and dealing with the obligations he had accumulated in connection with his school.(1) 'About a year ago,' he wrote before his execution, 'in view of the probability of my being arrested or of my losing my life either in the insurrection which I was then planning or otherwise in connection with my work as an Irish Volunteer, I wrote and deposited with my friend Mr Daniel Maher, Solicitor, Westland Row, Dublin, a short statement as to certain financial obligations of mine, which he was not to open except in the event of my death or arrest. As my life is now forfeited to British Law, he will shortly be free to open the document in question, and I desire him to do so; in the meantime I wish again to set down the substance of it, lest any accident should prevent the original document from being forthcoming.'(2) Nathan had no idea, as we said earlier, of the cleavage among the Volunteers and when, after the event, he rightly placed primary responsibility for the Rising on the I.R.B. he was unaware of the dominant position that Pearse, Plunkett, McDermott and Ceannt had achieved in that body. He, and his police advisers, had their eyes still on the old men, on T. J. Clarke of Dublin and John Daly of Limerick, what they called 'the small knot of violent men' who had been sentenced to penal servitude in 1883 in connection with the dynamite outrages of that time. These men, Nathan said, worked with great secrecy, never appearing on public platforms or in the press, or making themselves amenable to the law, all of which is true; but the initiative had long passed to other and younger men whose writing and speeches in favour of revolt were so common that they had come to believe that the Castle thought nothing of them.

Nathan was also at sea in thinking that the 'Castle Document' was fabricated in order to win popular sympathy for the Rising in the face of provocative action. The real reason, as we saw, was to provide the Volunteers with a justification for taking the initiative, and to deceive the MacNeill group. His crowning error, however, was to believe that Casement was to lead the Rising! 'On Easter Eve', he told the Royal Commission, 'the German ship was sunk, Sir Roger Casement who was to lead the Rising, had been captured and although these things were probably not wholly known to the Volunteer leaders, their Easter manoeuvres . . . had been cancelled. In these circumstances it was not believed that the threatened rising would take place. Generally, a rising either in the country or in Dublin except in support of an enemy that had landed, was looked upon as most improbable. Neither the strength, armament nor training of the Volunteers was of such a nature that seemed likely to promise to them such a measure of success as would lead them to make the attempt.' The latter part of that argument was undeniably sound, but Nathan was wrong in saying that Casement was to be leader of the Rising or that he was ever seen as likely to fill that role by any of his Irish colleagues. The exact opposite was the truth. Casement came home for the purpose of preventing the Rising or to say that if the Rising was contingent upon German help there were the gravest doubts as to its success. Nathan, however, was expressing the official British view which was based upon their Intelligence reports. Thus H. C. Hoy says that 'Germany's backing of Sir Roger Casement was a menace to be faced, and the Cabinet was acquainted with all the information Admiral Hall could give them. (This does not necessarily mean that he gave them all the information he had.) The date of the proposed rising was discovered, but there remained the all-important question of *when* Casement was to leave Germany', and, later, he speaks of the submarine being under orders to take Casement over to Ireland 'to start the Rebellion'. Room 40 O.B. eagerly awaited the signal of his departure. It came on 12 April and, said Hoy, 'our excitement at the Admiralty may be imagined'.(3)

Despite the limelight that surrounded him, Casement was at all times a secondary character in the play. He was not a member of the I.R.B. and did not suspect disunity among the Volunteers. If a rising was to take place he assumed that MacNeill would lead it. Joseph Plunkett did him the courtesy of announcing the Rising to him but the message conveyed through Plunkett's father from the German frontier, indicated that its source was the President and Supreme Council of the Irish Volunteers, which was confusing. President and Supreme Council were I.R.B. titles but Casement was intended possibly to believe that the message came from the President and Chief of Staff of the Irish Volunteers, MacNeill. He had gone to Germany on his own initiative and with his own ideas of what he should do while there and one of these things, the attempt to recruit an Irish Brigade from prisoners of war in German hands, was dubiously received in some Irish circles. Casement was distrusted on all sides for different reasons. He was regarded in Ireland and in America as an unpractical man to be sidetracked when serious business had to be done, and the Germans had independently come to the same conclusion. They preferred to work through Monteith when he was sent out to Germany and it was to Monteith they first divulged the information about the Rising. And Casement, beginning with the idea that the Germans were the *crème de la crème,* ceased to trust them, called them liars, and indulged in independent actions that vexed them. Behind their backs he sent a messenger to Ireland who was captured by the British and said to have been secretly executed.(4) The messenger, a Glasgow Irishman, John McGooey, had come from the United States to help the Brigade, and Casement sought to convey through him the details of the limited aid the Germans proposed to supply, as well as a warning along the lines that he himself tried to convey later in person. Casement did not know that the Clann na Gael and the I.R.B. people were satisfied to accept the limited German help. Through lack of information and different basic attitudes the Germans and the revolutionary Irish and Casement were at cross-purposes.

As for the British, to say that they distrusted Casement would be a gross understatement; to them he was a traitor and a lunatic capable of any folly. When he fell into their hands, it was inevitable that he would be found guilty of High Treason and put to death. They could not believe it possible that he had come back to Ireland to stop the Rising, and when this suggestion was put forward in the hope of securing a reprieve, it was officially and publicly denied.

Birrell cut a poor figure before the Royal Commission. He was vague and imprecise. He thought that if the Germans had succeeded in landing men as well as guns nobody would be able to say what an inflammable population might do; he had never been nervous about Ireland apart from a German landing of that sort, but he implied that this was not a serious possibility at Easter and that the rebels had fooled themselves by thinking that it was. They had swallowed the belief, too, he said, that England was surrounded by submarines, that the British could not move troops across the Channel. They believed that England was cut off and the moment they discovered that this was not so, that soldiers were in fact pouring in, they collapsed. He did not think it would have made any difference, except to the Germans, if Dublin had been held for another week.

He suggested that their general policy on the carrying of arms was at the root of the trouble. 'It may have been right or it may have been wrong,' he said, 'but it was part and parcel of a policy that we could not advisedly or properly or safely proceed by soldiers to disarm these men forcibly. It was the same thing which prevented us from acting in Ulster and I think rightly. You must bear in mind that we had the same policy (for both parts of the country).'

He admitted frankly that their Intelligence system had failed them, particularly that of the D.M.P. 'I always thought', he said, 'that I was very ignorant of what was actually going on in the minds, and in the cellars if you like, of the Dublin population. I was always exceedingly nervous about that. Therefore, I distinguished very much in my own mind between the state of things going on in Dublin and the state of things going on in the rest of the country. So far as Dublin is concerned, I do not know if Sir Matthew was more in a position than I was to receive these warnings, but I am not conscious of any until towards the end, 16 April, when we had that letter from Stafford to General Friend telling us about the ship ... I did hear at different times that there were notions that the Castle was going to be taken. Some steps I believe were taken to deal with these reports, which never came off. I should be very anxious to hear about them. I know it was all over Dublin that everybody knew this thing was going to happen ... I really am not aware of any warning beyond what I saw myself in the streets, and on that point I took very decided views ... I was very uncertain about Dublin'. He had told the military at a couple of conferences that he wanted more soldiers with bayonets and bands to be seen in Dublin 'because the impression that one gained in walking about the streets was as if the Sinn Féiners were in a certain sense in possession'. But the military were very busy training men for the Front and could not spare any for parades of that kind.

It was a common statement at this time that the D.M.P. was a less efficient force than the R.I.C., which was supposed to know everything that was happening in the country, and being armed and trained in the use of arms, could, with a military backing, take on any tumult that might be likely to occur. The D.M.P. was a different proposition – the shortcomings of its Intelligence Service (the G-Division) had been mentioned more than once in Nathan's time and of course it was in the D.M.P. area that the mischief which provoked the Rebellion was conceived. The D.M.P. were not an armed force either. Revolvers had been made available to some of the stations but the ordinary constable had not been shown how to use them which made him a greater danger to himself and to the general public than to a law breaker. When he was asked if his detective department had been more efficient, would not he have known about the Rising, he replied, 'Well, I am yet a little bit at a loss to know what precisely there was to know, . . .'. The rebels had kept their secrets to themselves. Generally, going back as far as Napper Tandy, the Government always had 'friends' in the rebel camp but, whether it was to the credit or discredit of the Sinn Féin movement, this was not now the case. Events showed that further assistance along the lines of a C.I.D. was required.

Wimborne made a fine showing when his turn came. It gave him an opportunity, of which he availed fully, to explain the anomalous position he was in; theoretically at the head of the Irish triumvirate but in fact the least powerful as well as the youngest of the three.

Friend, in his turn, did well in describing the difficulties he had before the Rising in carrying on with reduced forces, recognizing that their primary requirements was to raise recruits and only to draw on reinforcements from England in a case of real emergency. He was questioned, but not too closely because it was a delicate matter, about the warnings they had received, and about his own absence from Ireland without leave when the outbreak occurred. He had left on the evening of Good Friday. 'Wasn't that rather risky?' he was asked. Friend did not think so. He had heard of the capture of the boat before he started, and on Saturday morning at the Headquarters of the Home Forces where he had gone he was told of the ship having been sunk. He had a recollection of two or three occasions when Sir Matthew Nathan had demurred to his proposed action. In every such case, he thought it was not advisable to go on with the action. Sir Matthew acted on grounds of policy rather than on grounds of insufficient evidence. The Rising had taken him (Friend) by surprise. Beforehand he had thought the chief place of danger was the South rather than Dublin. When 'the Casement invasion' failed he thought the rising in the South would not take place.

Price, giving evidence, unlike Friend, was openly antagonistic to Birrell and Nathan without mentioning them by name. His position had been like that of John the Baptist, he said, a voice crying in the wilderness. He got in his dig at the Irish Party Leaders: in matters of policy it always struck him that the Irish Government were guided by the opinions of outsiders and not always by the opinions of their subordinates who supplied the information.

For the rest, the evidence weighed heavily against Birrell and Nathan, and Birrell became depressed. 'My dear Nathan,' he wrote, 'I think the Commission has got on to very boggy and untrustworthy ground, Ross, Harrell, O'Connell etc., and as these witnesses were not cross-examined I have no doubt that they have made quite a false impression as to their evidential value on the minds of the Commissioners, which is sure to find utterance in the report. . . . For some reasons I should like to be recalled but, *on reflection,* I don't think it would be dignified for me to wrangle with such persons, particularly as my criticism would have to be directed against the *weight* of the evidence and the *bias* of the men. So I must leave it alone. I asked whether I was wanted again and was told No, so I am crossing to France on Thursday night by Southampton and Havre. The whole *Dublin* Inquiry has been a meagre jejune performance, mere scratching the surface, but how could it be otherwise? Hardly a practical suggestion for safeguarding Dublin has emerged. I confess I thought *poorly* of them *all* but then as I think very poorly of myself, it doesn't carry one very far. We must expect a slating. I haven't heard whether R(edmond) and D(illon) mean to give evidence. The latter was thinking of it when I met him by *accident* in the cloakroom of the House.

Their line will be *they* could have done it safely enough. Their *conceit* is colossal. . . . The Irish papers are very hopeless reading. After Thursday I hope I shall never see them again – but I *suppose* there is just a chance of a patch up.

Well I hope you and I will always remain friends and have a sneaking kind of respect for each other, whatever the Commission or the press may say.

Yours always,
Augustine Birrell.'(5)

Nathan also had thought that he would have been re-examined, but when he learned on 2 June that he would not be wanted again he made no complaint. He just packed up the files he had assembled in preparing his evidence and returned them to Brennan with slips suggesting how they should be disposed of. One of them – it must have been a pretty big file – was Tom Clarke's and no doubt gave as good a picture as the police could put together of this quiet unassuming man who, from the day of his release in 1898 after fifteen years penal servitude, till the day he stood before the firing squad had radiated belief in the separatist ideal. His file was put carefully away, as were other odds and ends, including a letter of Darrel Figgis's that we would like to know more about.

In the course of tidying up Nathan got rid of two very special papers, of which unfortunately we have no copies. If we had, we would be nearer the solution of the mystery that surrounds the Director of Military Intelligence's tip off from that 'absolutely reliable source'. These were the one from Stafford to Friend which Friend gave Nathan on 17 April, and the other from Hall to Price which Price gave to Nathan on 24 April (Easter Monday) just before the outbreak. Nathan sent these two letters back to Friend on 22 May and told him that he had communicated the substance of the first and showed confidentially the second to Lord Hardinge, the Chairman of the Royal Commission.(6) Friend acknowledged Nathan's letter and words of appreciation, 'I feel myself entirely responsible for the course I took in military arrangements here – and I consider I was greatly helped in arriving at my decisions – by the information and advice you were always so ready to give me . . . I was free to act entirely on my own judgement; also holding a force in hand large enough, in my opinion, to come to the aid of the civil power – when called upon to do so'.(7)

There was absolutely no comfort in the Commission's report for either Birrell or Nathan, when it appeared towards the end of June. It declared that the main cause of the rebellion was an unchecked growth of lawlessness, and the fact that Ireland for several years had been administered on the principle that it was safer and more expedient to leave the law in abeyance, if collision with any faction could thereby be avoided. Such a policy was the negation of the cardinal rule of law which demands that the enforcement of law and the preservation of order should always be independent of political expediency. The importation of arms and the toleration of drilling first in Ulster and then in other districts created conditions which rendered possible the troubles in Dublin and elsewhere. The Government's reluctance to act was largely prompted by the pressure brought to bear by the Parliamentary representatives of the Irish people, and in Ireland itself there developed a widespread belief that no repressive measures would be undertaken by the Government against sedition. This led to a rapid increase of preparations for insurrection and was the immediate cause of the outbreak. The Commission exculpated the Lord Lieutenant. He was in no way answerable for the policy of the Government in a system that was anomalous in quiet times and almost unworkable in times of crisis. No blame attached to the Police chiefs either. From them the Government had abundant material on which they could have acted many months before the Rising was actually contemplated. Likewise the Military Authorities were not responsible. They had pointed out the general danger to the Irish Government but their warnings fell on unheeding ears. Birrell, as administrative head of the Government in Ireland, was held primarily responsible for the situation that was allowed to arise and the outbreak that occurred and Nathan, although commended for carrying out with the utmost loyalty the policy of the Government and of his immediate superior the Chief Secretary, was considered not to have sufficiently impressed upon the Chief Secretary, during Birrell's prolonged absences from Dublin, the necessity for more active measures to remedy the situation which in December he had described to Birrell as 'most serious and menacing'.(8)

161

CHAPTER SEVENTEEN

Nathan took away with him the good wishes of many people, for nobody could question the transparent honesty of the man and the genuine efforts he had made – though foolish they seemed to some – to keep the peace in Ireland otherwise than by coercion and to prepare the way for a native Government. Some of those who wrote to him took it for granted that he had no responsibility for what had happened. Hobhouse recalled Nathan's warnings of the developments of Sinn Féinism and remembered being so impressed about the possibilities that he spoke to both Birrell and Redmond, only to be assured by both that Nathan's fears were groundless and exaggerated. 'And now it has been shown that they were neither and that you have been the victim of the one's carelessness and laziness and of the other's preoccupation with the war. Redmond spoke very generously to me of your service to Ireland, of the very good work you did with preparation for Home Rule Government, and of the satisfaction and pleasure he had found in collaboration with you, and of his regrets at your withdrawal which he had done his best to prevent. This unhappy event will not of course be more than a momentary halt in your career.'

Starkie, the Education Commissioner, said that knowing the *damnosa hereditas* to which Nathan succeeded he always sympathized with him in his job in Ireland and it was to him a deeply felt sorrow that his relations with the Irish should have terminated so tragically. 'I don't think you need have any fear that your friends do not acquit you of all responsibility for the national catastrophe. We all feel that the burden must be placed on other shoulders. . . .' Headlam, the Treasury Remembrancer, told him that 'happily the world knows now that the tragedy is the result of your loyalty to the policy imposed upon you by the ineffable Birrell, about whom I have never concealed my opinion. Unfortunately we live in a squeamish age, or he would have been impeached and executed ... you have only reaped where they had sown : but you suffer and they escape.' The Civil Servants in the Castle, he added, were waiting to know their fate, but Headlam could not believe that after Redmond had shown his utter ignorance of modern Ireland, they would be handed over to him. Price, the Intelligence Officer, who would have shared these views, also regretted the resignation. Nathan had been a really good friend, and allowed him to express his views candidly on matters of importance. 'I am exceedingly sorry that you had not a free hand to set things right.'

There is nothing among Nathan's papers from the Irish party leaders or rank and file but James O'Connor, the volatile Solicitor General, whom they had helped into office, wrote to him. He assumed the policy was Nathan's own and the Jew Nathan he was tired saying was 'one of the best Christians I ever met'. 'If you failed in your task,' he told him, 'you failed where nobody could have succeeded. One horn of the dilemma was as sharp as the other – if not more so, as an Irishman ought to say. I thought I knew my countrymen, being a man of the people, reared with the people, and I came to the same conclusion as you did. But, had your conclusion been different, an opposite line of conduct might, and I think would have made matters still worse ... I live in hopes that you will yet come back to crown your work here. I say this in spite of my repugnance to English rule – a repugnance which is not diminished by the fact that your successor – an amiable courteous gentleman – gives everyone of us the impression that he looks on our race as an inferior race – without stability or morals!' Chalmers, Nathan's successor, had had the same effect on Sir Horace Plunkett. He had read Nathan's evidence and thought it a masterful statement of the essential facts and he had been quite able, he said, to read between the lines the explanations which Nathan's loyalty to his chief prevented him from giving. But he did not see how any member of the Irish Government could be blamed for not expecting the insurrection to break out on Easter Monday. The knowledge of the leaders that German assistance was not forthcoming and MacNeill's decision to postpone the outbreak made it at least ten to one that nothing would happen. The situation had been aggravated by the military executions; and he regretted more than he could say that his country and people should be deprived of the experience and understanding sympathy of Nathan at such a moment. 'Sir Robert Chalmers is, I am sure,' he wrote, 'a very clever man but I should consider it a waste of my time, and he would consider it a waste of his, if I were to propose to discuss the latest phase of the Irish question with him.'

Raymond Needham, who regarded it as much the greatest privilege of his official life to have worked under Nathan, said that Ireland as well as himself had lost an influence it could ill afford to spare. 'But it is a strange country,' he said, 'what is sympathy anywhere else is weakness here; firmness is tyranny; justice is blood-thirstiness; and generally great qualities appear to cancel themselves out in incompetence. Yet there is something "intriguing" about the country (in both senses of the word!) something fascinating and the thing one leaves with disgust at one moment, one returns to the next moment to try to snatch a secret. It is something like the golf swing. . . .'

This was the plaint of men who had worked very closely with him. Magill, Birrell's able personal secretary, told him that he was sure no one could have worked harder or more disinterestedly than Nathan did and if things turned out badly at the end he was satisfied that if Nathan had taken any other line the result would have been infinitely worse. He thought people were beginning to realize this, and he ended his note by wishing that he was 'out of it' himself. J. P. Crowly, an old Treasury man and an Irish Catholic to boot, wrote to express his sorrow that Nathan was leaving Ireland but in the estimation of those qualified to judge he was leaving without an inch of discredit. 'The public,' he said, 'without an idea in its head that does not come from the newspapers, conceive that if we had the right men and the right systems there would be no disasters, and that if an outbreak could have been foreseen it ought to have been prevented. Such is not the view of those who know the history of the world. The Irish Government of 1798 knew for a long time that the rebellion was hatching but they were not able to prevent it and their preventive measures were the proximate cause of its outbreak. The Press says that the Sinn Féiners ought not to have been allowed to parade in arms on St Patrick's Day but they could not have been prevented without risking a pitched battle, and then you would have been denounced for not leaving them alone.' The private secretary, Brennan, who had been on excellent terms with Nathan, tried to get a photograph from him for the Under-Secretary's room in the Castle, but Nathan refused to give him one, even when his successor said he would not allow his to be hung unless Nathan's went alongside it. It would not be fitting, he said. But it was on his conscience that he never went to see, and gave no help to, the Clongowes Boys' Club. 'I was pressed by many things in those last weeks but am sorry I omitted that one.'(1)

Among the letters that Nathan kept from this time was a characteristic one from George Bernard Shaw which must be reproduced in full :

10 Adelphi Terrace,
London, W.C.
4 May 1916.

My dear Sir Matthew,

I write this from Swanage but am returning here tomorrow.

I congratulate you on coming in for the best rebellion for 118 years, probably the last chance of such an experience. I do not apologize for having told you that Sinn Féin would not fight. It was the right thing to tell you, and the right thing for you to assume. Birrell in his agitation gave himself and his department away unnecessarily. It is no more possible to govern a country on the assumption that such a convulsion is possible than it is to walk about London on the assumption that every man you meet may shoot you – though he may. Once the rising of an armed force of any denomination was tolerated the Government had to take the extra risks that all governments run from armed populations. It is the merest chance that the rising was not made in Belfast by Carson's forces : a sham Popish plot as cleverly worked as the document about which Ginnell asked a question of T. W. Russell in the House would have done the trick. I have a copy of it; and it is quite plausible enough as evidence of a Castle plot to convince a Sinn Féiner.

Anyhow, Birrell's justification is clear – if only he saw it. He could not have provided against the danger except by impartially disarming the population as populations are normally disarmed in Italy, for example, where it is a criminal offence to carry weapons. As he was not enabled to do this, he was not in a position to conclude that any section of the population could run amok like lunatics. If you will not draw a dog's teeth you must allow him his first bite.

My report to you of my own proceedings is now of no interest. I wrote an article on Irish nonsense about Ireland and, to bribe the *New York Times* to insert it, I coupled with it a second article called *The American German's Case Against Germany*. The *New York Times* published them on 9 and 16 April. The *Irish Times* reprinted the Irish one on the 22nd. The immediate effect, apparently, was the rebellion. Hardly a success for my effort, that.

I am sorry, seeing that the three Manchester Martyrs were so nearly worn out, that they have been replaced. Nothing now can ever make those three tailors of Tooley Street ridiculous : their halos are safe for the next 100 years.

And why, oh why didn't the artillery knock down half Dublin whilst it had the chance? Think of the insanitary areas, the slums, the glorious chance of making a clean sweep of them! Only 179 houses and probably at least nine of them quite decent ones. I'd have laid at least 17,900 of them flat and made a decent town of it!

Yours sincerely,
G. Bernard Shaw.

Shaw in the next few days was protesting publicly against the policy of shooting the Sinn Féin prisoners first and telling the public about it afterwards. The men who were shot in cold blood after their capture or surrender were prisoners of war, and it was entirely incorrect to slaughter them. An Irishman was as much in order morally in accepting assistance from the Germans in his struggle with England as England was in accepting the assistance of Russia in her struggle with Germany. And he added, what was quickly demonstrated to be true, that it was impossible to slaughter a man in this position without making him a martyr and a hero. The shot Irishmen would now take their places beside Emmet and the Manchester Martyrs in Ireland ... Shaw was not a Sinn Féiner and he had used all his influence and literary power to discredit the Sinn Féin ideal,

and in particular to insist on the duty of Ireland to throw herself
with all her force on the side of the French Republic against
the Hohenzollern and Hapsburg monarchies. 'But I remain an
Irishman', he said, 'and am bound to contradict any implica-
tion that I can regard as a traitor any Irishman taken in a
fight for Irish independence against the British Government,
which was a fair fight in everything except the enormous odds
my countrymen had to face.'

And before he finished this contribution which helped to
ensure the ultimate popular success of the Rising, he added that
he thought it hard that Birrell, an Englishman, should be sacri-
ficed on the tombs of the fallen Sinn Féiners. 'Mr Birrell and
Sir Matthew Nathan did what they could with their hands tied
by the Army commands and Sir Edward Carson.'(2) This was
far from being the truth, however.

George Russell (AE) wrote to Nathan. They had met occasionally in Dublin, probably through the Horace Plunketts with
whose co-operative interests AE was connected. AE had told
him of his campaigning through the *Irish Homestead*, of which
he was editor, for higher standards, particularly of honesty
which they agreed was what Ireland needed most. A link between them was the group of Irish literary men who had gone
to the war – Patrick Magill, novelist become rifleman, and
Francis Ledwidge, poet and lance-corporal in the Inniskillings,
as well as Lord Dunsany, Stephen Gwynn, and Canon Hannay
(George Birmingham). But one suspects that as a guide to the
realities of Irish life AE was anything but sound. He had, for
instance, in October 1915 approved of his publishers authoris-
ing the Countess Markievicz to use his poems. She was, he said,
an enthusiastic lady who believed in boy scouts and wanted to
combine poetry and scouting and make her boys into poets
as well as heroes. 'I don't think her experiment will be a success, but I wish it well and I like the idea of boy scouts with a
pocket book of poetry, so please let them try.' The uniformed
Countess brandishing a revolver had become the most fabulous
figure in the Rising and two of her Fianna boys had been
executed! However, AE now told Nathan that he only wished
he were staying. 'You are the only official who has come to
Ireland who seemed as much a human being as an officer of
state and I think that your policy of not antagonising the

extremists was right and if you had not had your hand forced would have succeeded in carrying us through the war without a conflict in Ireland. I don't believe an insurrection was thought of seriously by any except a small group of volunteers. They had determined, of course, to resist conscription and disarming but they had no activities contemplated in the nature of a revolt saving that very small group represented by Clarke and Connolly . . .' The document read by Alderman Kelly might have been forged as a joke and passed out just to see what the effect would be. If so, Heaven forgive the scoundrel who did it. It enabled the extremists to work on the feelings of the passive resisters. 'But perhaps,' he went on, 'it was all inevitable from the moment the Ulster men armed and gave the extremists here the chance of arming and drilling too. I wish to say that you carry away with you the goodwill of many people who never regretted the departure of a Chief or Under-Secretary of Ireland before . . . I am very sad over Ireland just now. I knew many of those now dead and had a genuine liking for them. They had no intellect. Connolly was the only one with a real grip on his mind. They were rather featherbrained idealists, . . .*, and now they will be national heroes. If I had remembered Connolly was in the counsels of the Irish Volunteers I would have been frightened. He lay low, and I believe he cast the torch on the pile. Goodbye and good luck. I will always feel you were a friend of Ireland no matter what the political bigots say'.

Nathan replied:

'Your letter gave me pleasure by the kindliness of the feeling it showed towards me and the satisfactory views it expressed as to the policy I adopted in Ireland. Though of course it is impossible to contend in the face of events that that policy did not fail, I still think that the error of placing too low the limits of human folly and being insufficiently prepared for these limits being exceeded was a lesser one – even in its effects, disastrous as they were – than would have been the alternative of a rigid suppression of a movement which would have widened and intensified the feeling that

*Two names are written here. The first seems to be Pearse; the second is indecipherable.

gave rise to it. I believe I was in the main right in making great allowances for Irish aspirations in the belief that in time it will be found possible to get Irishmen to accept a realisation of these aspirations consistent with the maintenance of a British connection required alike for the safety of England and the material (and I believe also the moral) welfare of Ireland.

I still look forward to the national movements, which of late have thought it necessary to get popularity by associating their aims with those of the political extremists, becoming again independent, and of a love of Ireland being dissociated from a hatred of my country. This last is something for which it is worth while for the writers and thinkers of Ireland to work and I believe you will work for it.'(3)

Canon Hannay wrote to him from Boulogne where he was serving as an Army chaplain. Nathan's departure would be a personal loss. He had greatly enjoyed their intercourse in Dublin, but he was more sorry that Nathan was leaving Ireland for the sake of his poor country. 'I am convinced that you would have done much good in Ireland if you had stayed. Alas, saddest of all are the circumstances of your going. I look forward with dread to the reviving of the old bitterness and hatred; and to the setting in our people's minds of a fresh burden of miserable memories. Our star is surely, of all, the most malignant . . .'(4)

He had a message from Dorothy Stopford. She had gone up to the Under-Secretary's Lodge to take away the things she had left behind on that exciting Easter Monday and learned that Sir Matthew was gone. She had wanted to tell him how horrible it had been of the house party to leave before he came back, 'rude and ungracious . . . but I couldn't help it any more than you could your second disappearance. It has been a terrible time', she continued, 'and now as a culminating blow you are going. If every one, Irish and English, had worked for Ireland as you have done, perhaps the unhappy country would have found some contentment before now. Your policy was too good for some of them, and you yourself as I always said were much too good for that abominable post . . .'(5)

This letter was to Nathan 'a bright spot in a dark time'. He told Dorothy that he would try not to go back to Ireland, 'not to see again the land I had hoped and failed to help'. But he would like to be informed of 'any good to Ireland, and to England and Ireland coming out of all the losses and sufferings of that week between St George's Day and May Day ....' A few months later he was telling her how glad he was to hear that Mrs Green was keeping out of mischief, and hoping that T. P. Gill would be made Under-Secretary. 'I think his characteristics are all the exact opposite to mine so that he ought to succeed'. Gill did not get the post but the man who was appointed, Sir William P. Byrne, was both an Irishman and a Catholic which was a step, Nathan said, in the right direction. His own assistant, Sir Edward O'Farrell, would have answered those requirements but it was not in him, Nathan said, to take responsibility so he doubted if he would have accepted the post. He hoped the new man would be given a fair chance in Ireland from whence he had heard nothing satisfactory for some time past. 'I saw *John Bull's Other Island* acted in London four or five years ago,' he said 'and afterwards read the play very carefully. It is a comedy setting forth very truly the Irish tragedy, for tragedy it is in Martha's sight whatever it may be to the eyes of Mary.'

He kept up his reading about Ireland, the newspapers, of course, and AE's writings. Susan Mitchell on George Moore intrigued him, but nothing more than James Stephens on the Rebellion. Before he had a copy of the book he was glad to see from the press notices that it was written with a conciliatory and not with an inflammatory aim which was the usual thing.(6)

Mrs Green was also among the leave-takers. She had been one of those to whom a copy of the document alleged to have been taken from the files of Dublin Castle had been sent before the Rising and she had 'ventured to be reckless' by inviting Nathan for his comment on it. 'If it is correct,' she said, 'we should soon see irremediable trouble. If it is fancy it shows the state of nerves of the Volunteers.' That was on the 23 April (Easter Sunday), and Nathan had resigned before he could write to her; in the meantime an official reply had been given to the question in the House of Commons. Nathan, however, on the 13 May gave Mrs Green a personal assurance – 'no such document nor any similar document was or had been in existence on the files of Dublin Castle or elsewhere. I find that what purported to be a decipher of this imaginary document was circulated to many people of position in Irish affairs. You may be able to judge what was the wicked purpose of this'.(7) It was more than a fortnight after this that she wrote her first post-Rising letter to Nathan. She had tried to write earlier but 'there was no use trying. I was too broken-hearted'. Some of the people she knew and admired had been involved in the Rising and were now either dead or imprisoned. Her closest companion in the movement, Casement, was very obviously destined for the gallows; and from his prison cell he had told her of the hopelessness of the Rising and of his failure to prevent it. She was working desperately hard now to save his life, helping to organise, and to find funds for, his legal defence and appealing to influential persons to bring pressure to bear on the Government. In the process she had brought renewed suspicion on herself and the police had searched her house. But there was no word of this as she reviewed the position for Nathan. 'I don't take back anything I have said or wrote to you,' she said, 'I only wish that I had told you more of my own experience and knowledge ... I saw your devoted work. I was deeply conscious the last time I stayed with you of your growing sense of what Ireland meant and how it should be redeemed. Your devotion to public duty was conspicuous and admirable. Alas! I have seen others broken by a monstrous system against which all zeal and ability seems vain.

What an ignominy for any Government in a civilised country to have as its one resource always an unashamed coercion and martial law! It is not care for Ireland but to save the face of England that that solution is proposed now. The problem is given to a man who never cared one farthing or knew one fact about Ireland. So we have by order infinite hopes and unbounded loyalty.

I can't say to you now the things I believe, and I esteem you far too much to say nothing. Perhaps the time may come when this madness is over. I may keep anger to some whom you respect but I have always admired your devoted and self-sacrificing work.'(8)

Nathan had not expected to hear from Mrs Green so soon for he told her 'I was fully conscious of all you must be suffering and of the difficulty of writing in the midst of your sorrow. I realised that in addition to your feelings for Ireland in which, though of course on a different plane, I had participation, you had deep grief for persons who for me were only names associated with the ends I tried to prevent. Believe me that you have my heartfelt sympathy.

I also have nothing to take back from what I said to you; I wish I had. I remember in one or two of those pleasant walks to the Parkgate telling you that my great fear, to prevent which was the one aim of my work, was that some action of the anti-British in Ireland during the war would set back the growing English sympathy for your country. My fear was justified and my work a failure.

Now I am going back to my old Corps and to much the same sort of duty that I was doing in the days before I first met you. But I am not without confidence in the much shorter future before me and with many regrets for what has happened in the recent past have no remorse for my part in it'.(9)

That letter filled Mrs Green with admiration. In all kinds of unexpected ways she heard of the impression that Nathan's work and devotion made on the rank and file of people in Ireland. He was steadily gaining confidence and respect, in spite of the first clamour, and in telling him this she was glad to think that the people were intelligent enough, and just enough, and candid enough to recognize able, loyal and sincere service. She was glad to be at one with her people in this estimate, with the obscure ones who had no newspapers to speak for them. Those were the ones she cared for.(10) But one wonders did the ordinary people of Ireland, or of England for the matter of that, think in this fashion of Nathan. Or ever even heard of him. But the warmhearted 'widow Green' genuinely felt that way herself. She kept up her friendship with the ex-Under-Secretary and reminded him from time to time of her belief that the Government's action in getting rid of him and Birrell was a cowardly outrage that filled her with the greatest indignation. She plied him with her opinions on men and matters and questioned the sources of his information. Thus on the 25 January 1917, she told him she saw in questions he had asked her – presumably about literature in the Irish language – the trail of Mahaffy, the Provost of Trinity College, or those who had learned from him, the most malign influence in Ireland. 'He has the pose of the learned man, and the vulgarity of a man who thinks that there is no shame in blazoning out his ignorance and mocking at the learning he does not know. I know the effect he has produced on Scandinavian scholars who came to Ireland, but unfortunately the Irish level of intelligence has been too much degraded to give public feeling there a real efficiency in showing up his ignorance at its true worth. You will forgive this outburst. I don't know Irish, but I do know the people who know it, and I do at least ask them questions'. And she ended that particular letter by saying something which, without her knowing or wishing it, reflected on the person to whom she was writing. 'What an amazing thing it is', she said, 'that in the centuries of English rule there has never been sent over a single man who had any knowledge of the Irish tradition, history, monuments or memories. Surely that mere fact is enough to explain continual disaster. Mr Birrell had intuitions, but he could go no further. He scarcely knew indeed himself what they meant, but it touched me to see that they were there.'(*11*)

CHAPTER EIGHTEEN

Nathan was rather sentimental about his birthdays, and had celebrated the one that fell on 3 January 1916 by inviting to dine with him Mrs Constance Heppell-Marr, the daughters as was mentioned earlier, of an Assistant Secretary in the Irish Department of Agriculture and Technical Instruction. She was a petite, fair-haired, good-looking, clever young lady with a good carriage and plenty of character, the sort of person who has been described as 'full of herself' and 'in everything' philanthropic. She may also have been something of a social climber. At any rate, it was said that her wedding was more noted for the fact that Lady Aberdeen, the Viceroy's wife, came to it than for anything else. The marriage was not a great success, and when the war came Constance left her two young children in the care of a governess and busied herself with war work. She became the Honorary Secretary of the Irish Branch of the British Red Cross Society and it may have been in this capacity that she first met Nathan. She had already corresponded with him about her husband, a colliery manager at Castlecomer, who had joined an infantry regiment but wanted a transfer to the Royal Engineers. She was 'uncommonly lonely lately', she told Nathan, so that dinner in the Under-Secretary's Lodge, at which she sang for him, was 'a delightful experience' and encouraged her to ask him to dine with her in a 'top-back' in Lower Baggot Street to which she was moving. He could come straight from the office and there would be a room where he could change. One wonders if anybody in Baggot Street, Upper or Lower, dresses nowadays for dinner?

Constance emerged from the Rising with distinction. She organized a hospital, attended to the wounded in the streets under fire, and brought supplies through the firing line regardless of danger. For these services she was awarded a silver medal by the Order of St John of Jerusalem. But she told Nathan, who by this time had left Dublin, that all was dust and ashes, and that she would rather wash dishes in England than remain in Ireland. She wrote these words as she prepared to attend 'an idiotic review' where she would be told that she was a brave woman for doing, with the protection of her 'silly uniform', what many a servant maid did unprotected. In order to bespeak his interest, presumably, she told Nathan that a friend of hers, Margaret MacNeill, would probably forfeit her post as Inspectress of Industrial Schools for being a sister of the head of the Irish Volunteers. This would mean disaster for the children of another member of the MacNeill family whom she supported. It was terrible, Constance said, to see a great and brave soul torn to shreds. Miss MacNeill retained her post.

Before the war was over Mrs Heppell-Marr's correspondence with Nathan ceased. She re-married and achieved something like fame as Constance Spry; her work as a floral decorator and as the founder of a rather unique school in Berkshire certainly made her well-known.

A close friendship grew up between Nathan and Amber Blanco White, which also petered out after over thirty years, and Amber looked back on their association with cold detachment. She told the present author that she had met Nathan on some committee or other when she was in the Ministry of Labour and he in Pensions. He was a dear, charming, impressive-looking man, but a philanderer, a man who thought women existed to serve him; a bit of a humbug too, she thought, and not very sincere. He had talked to her about his past, his engineering feats, his colonial government experience, and about Ireland. From being 'the star of the Civil Service' he had been degraded but the many friends he had taken pains to cultivate rallied round and put him back in the firmament.

CHAPTER NINETEEN

Nathan waited until the Royal Commission closed its sittings before reporting for duty to the Military Authority. He was then employed in a manner that befitted a person in disgrace although that may not have been intended. He was sent as staff officer to the Chief Engineer, London Defences, and for five months helped to prepare for an invasion of England in which no one greatly believed, supervizing the throwing up of earth-works on positions North and South of the Thames by volunteers unfit for active service. Concurrently he served on a Home Office Committee that sought to find useful employment for conscientious objectors. 'I do mind dreadfully', he told Dorothy Stopford, 'that it should be so futile, that for four months now I should have been in the minority that is not really helping the country. . . . They are a queer lot – those with religious scruples as a rule behave very well and those with political scruples, badly. My other job . . . is still more pointless' (25 September 1916). But in November 1916 his luck turned and he resumed his long series of distinguished assignments. He was first nominated to be Secretary of the new War Pensions Department and entered with customary zest into this new field. He did not find his mind often dwelling now on Ireland and its problems; nor could he be of service in solving them.(1) Nevertheless, he was deeply interested. The war continued to go badly and he learned from a conversation à trois with Lloyd George and Carson that there would have to be a good deal of setting of the national teeth and square facing of the national difficulties before these could be overcome. Manpower was still a vital problem, and the possibility of enforcing conscription in Ireland remained. He availed of his meeting with Carson in February 1917 to put a point he had always felt, 'that if the Unionists had answered Redmond's appeal in the first days of

176

the War a wave of enthusiasm might have swept over Ireland and sent many murky memories into the dust bin of oblivion'.(2)

In the early days of 1918 he discussed with Horace Plunkett and George Barnes, the Labour Minister, the state of the negotiations for a settlement of the Irish question. It looked at that time, however, that any agreement that might be reached would have to be forcibly enforced from outside which, Nathan reflected, was not a very hopeful augury for future peace inside. In April of that year Plunkett was taking as serious a view as Dorothy Stopford did of the effects of imposing conscription in Ireland and was hoping that it could be staved off. A national pledge was taken to resist it. He knew nothing himself from the inside of what the Government proposed to do and he was unable therefore to intervene in any way as Miss Stopford had apparently suggested. 'I must not forget,' he told her, 'that after my year and a half in Ireland in which I advised against conscription – which advice was then taken – and for conciliatory treatment, advice that was so far followed that rebellion had to be prepared by a lying pamphlet – a rebellion did come, with the inevitable "I told you so" from the reactionaries and not *one* word said *for* the policy by the Irish! It is not from bitterness that I refer to this but to show that for men to offer advice not asked for would be not only ineffectual but might not unreasonably be held to be impertinent. In the meantime I am glad that the pledge was taken on St George's Day and so like the rebellion which broke out on the same day cannot be effectual.'

Three years later he became Governor of Queensland and Chancellor of the University there. In the last few years before retirement he served on a special commission on the Constitution of Ceylon and then as Chairman of the Colonial Secretary's advisory committee on rubber. In retirement he interested himself in the administration of the County of Somerset and in local history on which he became an authority of some consequence. He was a Vice-President of the Royal Geographical Society from 1929 to 1932, and for many years a contributor of reviews to its journal. At a later date he became a Fellow of the Society of Antiquarians and of the Royal Historical Society. He did not live to see the publication of a monumental work of his on the annals of West Coker where he spent his last years but, typically, in completing the book he had added a preface in which he acknowledged his great gain in pleasure and interest from a work to which he had turned when these could no longer be drawn from the public positions it had been his good fortune to occupy.(3) To the end he was the conscientious servant of the public and deserves to be remembered as such.

Though he appears to have kept his promise never to go back to Ireland he was always glad to hear about the country, and about the people who had shared his interest in its welfare. One day in 1937 Bernard Shaw was brought to see him at West Coker. 'This was for Shaw one of the happiest engagements we made for him', St John Ervine wrote. 'Just why it gave him so much pleasure I do not know, except, perhaps, that it gave him a chance to talk about Ireland.'(4) But it was no less happy for Nathan for the same reason, although, being English, he could see a second side to the Anglo-Irish relations problem and was always anxious lest that side should be overlooked or under-estimated. This emerges very clearly from the letter he sent to Dorothy Stopford when her aunt, Mrs Green, died in 1929 full of honours from the Irish Free State of which she had become a much-esteemed Senator. 'We had been friends since we foregathered at the beginning of the century in our apprecia-tion of Mary Kingsley', he told her, 'and she tried to help me when I was in Ireland and understood the lines of my ineffectual work there. . . . I should immensely like to have you and your husband here so that when you do bring yourself to come again to visit this oppressive, wicked, effete and in every way abomin-able England, you must come to me and learn to change your opinions or at any rate some of them.' In his opinion the re-education of Dorothy was necessary because, like the majority of the Irish people, her thinking had been transformed by the failure of the 1916 rebellion and the triumph of the ideals of the men who made it.

Nathan died on 18 April 1939.

REFERENCES

CHAPTER TWO

1. Sir Matthew Nathan, *Annals of West Coker*, xiii, Cambridge, 1937.
1a. Violet Bonham Carter, *Winston Churchill As I Knew Him*, London, 1965, p. 380.
2. Olwen Ward Campbell, *Mary Kingsley*, London, 1957, p. 171.
3. Maurice Headlam, *Irish Reminiscences*, London, 1947, pp. 37–8.
4. *The Leader*, 21 November 1914.
5. Ibid., 10 October 1914.
6. Nevil Shute, *Slide Rule*, London, 1954, p. 13.
7. MS. Nathan 409: Norway to Nathan, 30 September 1914.
8. Sir Henry Robinson, *Memories, Wise and Otherwise*, London, 1923, p. 223.
9. Augustine Birrell, *Things Past Redress*, London, 1937, p. 206.
10. Ibid., p. 196.
11. MS. Nathan 462: Nathan to Lloyd George, 12 October 1914.
12. Birrell, op. cit., p. 215.

CHAPTER THREE

1. Birrell, op. cit., pp. 216–17.
2. Emmet Larkin, *James Larkin*, London, 1965, p. 182.
3. R. Barry O'Brien, *Dublin Castle and the Irish People*, London, 1909, p. 33.
4. MS. Nathan 449: Birrell to Nathan, 14 February 1915.
5. Leslie Byron, *Opportunist Sinn Féiners*, London, 1921, p. 103.

CHAPTER FOUR

1. MS. Nathan 462: 11 November 1914.
2. MS. Norway: 'Irish Experiences in War', p. 6.
3. MS. Nathan 449: Birrell to Nathan, 2 November 1914.
4. MS. Nathan 462: Nathan to Birrell, 3 November 1914.
5. MS. Nathan 449: Birrell to Nathan, 18 December 1914.
6. Ibid., 25 or 28 December 1914.

7. Ibid., 26 December 1914.
8. Geoffrey de G. Parmiter, *Roger Casement,* London, 1936, p. 183.
9. Ibid., p. 192.
10. Darrell Figgis, *Recollections of the Irish War,* London, 1927, pp. 72–8.
11. Sir William M. James, *The Eyes of the Navy,* London, 1955, chap. III.
12. Figgis, op. cit., p. 77.
13. MS. Nathan 462: Nathan to Birrell, 30 December 1914.
14. Ibid., Nathan to Norway, 25 and 27 January 1915.
15. Ibid., 4 January 1915.
16. *An Claidheamh Soluis,* 1 November 1913.
17. Documents relative to the Sinn Féin Movement, 1921.
18. MS. Nathan 449: Birrell to Nathan, 2 December 1914.
19. Ibid., 14 December 1914.
20. MS. Nathan 471: Notebook.
21. MS. Nathan 449: Birrell to Nathan, 22 December 1914.

CHAPTER FIVE

1. MS. Nathan 462: Nathan to Birrell, 9 November 1914.
2. Ibid., Norway to Nathan, 26 November 1914.
3. Ibid., Nathan to Hobhouse, 6 December 1914.
4. Ibid., 20 December 1914.
5. MS. Nathan 454–5: Hobhouse to Nathan, 25 December 1914.
6. MS. Nathan 462: Nathan to Norway, 4 January 1915.
7. Ibid., 21 January 1915.
8. Norway, op. cit., p. 10.
9. Ibid., pp. 12–14.

CHAPTER SIX

1. J. A. Froude, *History of England,* London, 1862, 3rd edition revised, vol. II, chap. IX, p. 341.
2. MS. Nathan 465: Nathan to Redmond, 9 December 1915.
3. MS. Nathan 460–1: Selbourne to Nathan, 30 November 1914.
4. MS. Nathan 454–5: Long to Nathan, 21 April 1915.
4a. MS. Nathan 50: 1915 Diary.
5. MS. Nathan 462: Nathan to Birrell, 18 February 1915.
6. Ibid., Nathan to Dillon, 3 March 1915.
7. Ibid., Nathan to Birrell, 20 October 1914.
8. MS. Nathan 450–1: Dillon to Nathan, 7 December 1914.
9. MS. Nathan 449: Birrell to Nathan, 8 September 1915.
10. Ibid., 28 December 1914.
11. Loc. cit.
12. MS. Nathan 462: Police Report, 5 November 1914.
13. MS. Nathan 449: Police Report, undated.

14. Ibid., 8 February 1915.
15. MS. Nathan 450–1: Dillon to Nathan, 21 February 1915.
16. MS. Nathan 462: Nathan to Dillon, 22 February 1915.
17. MS. Nathan 50: 1915 Diary.

CHAPTER SEVEN

1. MS. Nathan 449: Birrell to Nathan, 12 June 1915.
1a. Haldane Papers. MS. 5912 f. 11, 2 June 1915.
2. Denis Gwynn, *The Life of John Redmond,* London, 1931, p. 446.
3. MS. Nathan 464: Nathan to Birrell, 2 September 1915.
4. MS. Nathan 454–5: Edgeworth-Johnstone to Nathan, 29 July 1915.
5. MS. Nathan 464: Nathan to Dillon, 22 July 1915.
6. Ibid., Nathan to Birrell, 31 July 1915.
7. MS. Nathan 465: Nathan to Kurten, 7 October 1915.
8. Gwynn, op. cit., p. 459.
9. Royal Commission, *On the Rebellion in Ireland,* London, 1916. Evidence, p. 29.
10. MS. Nathan 479: Note of interview of 14 December 1915 produced to Royal Commission.
11. MS. Nathan 465: Nathan to Birrell, 12 December 1915.
12. Ibid., Nathan to Sir Nugent Everard, 7 October 1915.
13. Ibid., Nathan to A. P. Magill, 9 October 1915.
14. Ibid., Nathan to Dillon, 13 November 1915.
15. Ibid., Nathan to Birrell, 21 October 1915.
16. MS. Nathan 466: Nathan to Birrell, 4 January 1916.
16a. 'Ireland and the First World War' in *The Matter with Ireland,* ed. by D. H. Greene and D. H. Laurence, 1962; and MS. Eng. Lett. E. 100, 29 November 1914.
17. St John Ervine, *Bernard Shaw,* London, 1956, p. 47.
18. MS. Nathan 465: Nathan to George Bernard Shaw, 23 November 1915.
19. MS. Nathan 450–1: Brennan to Nathan, 22 November 1915.
20. MS. Nathan 469: Memorandum of Interview, 20 November 1915.
21. MS. Nathan 50: 1915 Diary.

CHAPTER EIGHT

1. MS. Nathan 466: Nathan to Birrell, 4 January 1916.
2. MS. Nathan 409: O'Farrell to Nathan, 1 December 1915.
3. Gerald French, *Life of Sir John French,* London, 1931, p. 338.
4. MS. Nathan 466: Nathan to Birrell, 18 February 1916.
5. Ibid., Nathan to Dillon, 15 March 1916.
6. MS. Nathan 450–1: Dillon to Nathan, 14 March 1916.
7. MS. Nathan 466: Nathan to Birrell, 18 March 1916.
8. Ibid., 24 March 1916.

9. Royal Commission, op. cit., p. 29.
10. MS. Nathan 466: Nathan to Birrell, 13 April 1916.
11. Royal Commission, op. cit., p. 32.

CHAPTER NINE

1. MS. Nathan 488: Wimborne to Nathan, 19 June 1915.
2. MS. Nathan 464: Nathan to Wimborne, 16 June 1915.
3. MS. Nathan 466: Nathan to Wimborne, 16 March 1916.
4. The Irish Times, *Sinn Féin Rebellion Handbook, Easter, 1916,* Dublin, 1917, p. 6.
5. MS. Nathan 472: Notebook.
6. MS. Nathan 466: Nathan to Birrell, 25 March 1916.
7. MS. Nathan 472: Notebook.
8. MS. Nathan 466: Nathan to Birrell, 4 April 1916.
9. Ibid., Nathan to Wimborne, 7 April 1916.
10. Ibid., Nathan to Birrell, 13 April 1916.
11. MS. Nathan 448: Wimborne to Nathan, 4 March 1916.
12. MS. Nathan 472: Notebook.
13. MS. Nathan 476, vol. I: Alice S. Green to Nathan, 14 April 1916.
14. Ibid., Nathan to Birrell, 24 March 1916.
15. Ibid., 7 April 1916.
16. Ibid., Nathan to Norway, 30 March 1916 and 13 April 1916.
17. Ibid., 6 April 1916.
18. Royal Commission, op. cit., p. 87.
19. MS. Nathan 466: Nathan to Birrell, 4 April 1916.
20. MS. Nathan 450–1: Dillon to Nathan, 13 April 1916.
21. MS. Nathan 466: Nathan to Birrell, 13 April 1916.
22. Royal Commission, op. cit., p. 113.
23. MS. Nathan 466: Nathan to Birrell, 4 April 1916.
24. Ibid., 7 April 1916.

CHAPTER TEN

1. MS. Nathan 466: Nathan to Birrell, 22 April 1916.
2. *The Drogheda Independent,* 22 April 1916.
3. MS. Nathan 466: Nathan to Grimwood Meares, 1 June 1916.
4. Gwynn, op. cit., p. 471.
5. MS. Nathan 466: Nathan to Birrell, 22 April 1916.
6. Ibid., Nathan to Anderson, 22 April 1916.
7. Countess of Fingal, *Seventy Years Young,* London, 1937, pp. 371–2.

CHAPTER ELEVEN

1. Royal Commission, op. cit., p. 63.
2. MS. Nathan 466: Nathan to Birrell, 24 April 1916.

3. Dep. Asquith 42: Memorandum prepared for Prime Minister.
4. MS. Nathan 449: Birrell to Nathan, 24 April 1916.
5. Headlam, op. cit., pp. 166–7.
6. MS. Nathan 51: Diary 1916.
7. Gwynn, op. cit., pp. 474–5.
8. MS. Nathan 51: Diary 1916.

CHAPTER TWELVE

1. MS. Nathan 476: Estelle Nathan to her husband, Easter Week, 1916.

CHAPTER THIRTEEN

1. Dep. Asquith 36: French to Prime Minister, 25 April 1916.
2. Ibid., Redmond to Prime Minister, 27 April 1916.
3. French, op. cit., p. 339.
4. Dep. Asquith 36: Lord Stamfordham to Bonham Carter, 27 April 1916.
5. Ibid., Maxwell to Prime Minister, 12 May 1916.
6. Sir John Maxwell's despatch, 25 May 1916.
7. Dep. Asquith 36: Birrell to Prime Minister, 28 April 1916.
8. Ibid., 29 April 1916.
9. Ibid., 30 April 1916.
10. Ibid., Prime Minister to Birrell, 1 May 1916.
11. J. A. Spender and Cyril Asquith, *Life of Lord Oxford and Asquith,* London, 1932, vol. II, p. 214.
12. Birrell, op. cit., pp. 219–21.
13. John Evelyn Wrench, *Struggle 1914–1920,* London, 1935, p. 207,
14. MS. Nathan 466: Nathan to Birrell, 11 May 1916.
15. Ibid., Nathan to Friend, 22 May 1916.
16. Gwynn, op. cit., pp. 476–7.
17. Ibid., p. 487.
18. D. Lynch and F. O'Donoghue, *The I.R.B. and the 1916 Insurrection,* Cork, 1957, pp. 21, 78, 81, 106, 159–61, and 183; and *An tOglách,* Christmas, 1962.
19. Gwynn, op. cit., p. 478.
20. Dep. Asquith 36: Pearse to Asquith, 7 May 1916.
21. Loc. cit.

CHAPTER FOURTEEN

1. French, op. cit., p. 341.
2. Dep. Asquith 36: Chalmers to Prime Minister, 9 May 1916.
3. French, op. cit., p. 340.
4. Ibid., pp. 340–1.

5. Fingal, op. cit., p. 375.
6. Gwynn, op. cit., pp. 482–4 and 489.
7. Dep. Asquith 43: G.O.C. Dublin to War Office, 29 May 1916.
8. MacNeill Papers.
9. Dep. Asquith 43: folio 5.
10. Ibid., Maxwell to Prime Minister, 21 May 1916.
11. Ibid.
12. Ibid., Dillon to Prime Minister, 21 May 1916.
13. Ibid., Maxwell to Bonham Carter, 26 May 1916.
14. Spender and Asquith, op. cit., pp. 216–17.
15. Dep. Asquith 44: 17 May 1916.
16. MS. Nathan 466: Nathan to Plunkett, 1 June 1916.
17. Dep. Asquith 44: Duke to Wimborne, 7 August 1916.
18. Dep. Asquith 43: folio 182.
19. Dep. Asquith 44: Maxwell to French, 13 May 1916.
20. Dep. Asquith 42: Maxwell to French, 16 June 1916.

CHAPTER FIFTEEN

1. John Bulloch, *M.I.5: Origin and History of British Counter-Espionage Service,* London, 1963, p. 188.
2. MS. Nathan 466: Nathan to Birrell, 22 April 1916.
3. Command 1108 of 1921.
4. H. C. Hoy, *40 O.B. or How the War Was Won,* London, 1932, p. 35.
5. James, op. cit., p. 169.
6. Admiral Sir Lewis Bayly, *Pull Together!* London, 1939, pp. 202–6.
7. John Devoy, *Recollections of an Irish Rebel,* New York, 1929, p. 403.
8. F. X. Martin, O.S.A., 'MacNeill on the 1916 Rising', *Irish Historical Studies,* (Dublin), XII No. 47 (March, 1961), 241.
9. Lynch and O'Donoghue, op. cit., p. 131 et seq.
10. Ibid., p. 47.
11. Ibid., p. 113.
12. James Connolly, *Labour and Easter Week,* Dublin, 1949, p. 9; and Martin, op. cit., p. 253.
13. Luigi Sturzo, 'Le Droit de Révolte et Ses Limites', *La Vie Intellectuelle* (Paris), LII, No. 2 (25 October, 1937), pp. 165 et seq.
14. Martin, op. cit., pp. 228–9.
15. Desmond Ryan, *The Rising,* Dublin, 1949, pp. 79–80; Dorothy MacArdle, *The Irish Republic,* Dublin, 1937, pp. 155–7; F. O'Donoghue, *Tomás MacCurtain,* Tralee, 1958, pp. 64–5.
16. Martin, op. cit., p. 252.
17. Connolly, op. cit., p. 18.
18. Ibid., p. 16; and Liam O'Briain, *Cuimhni Cinn,* Dublin, 1951, pp. 162–3.
19. Connolly, op. cit., p. 21.
20. MS. Nathan 466: Nathan to Birrell, 11 May 1916.
21. MacNeill Papers.

CHAPTER SIXTEEN

1. Dep. Asquith 43.
2. Ibid.
3. Hoy, op. cit., p. 134 et seq.
4. Wm. J. Maloney, *The Forged Casement Diaries,* Dublin, 1936, pp. 253–4.
5. MS. Nathan 449.
6. Ibid., Nathan to Friend, 22 May 1916.
7. Ibid., Friend to Nathan, 24 May 1916.
8. Royal Commission, op. cit., pp. 12–14.

CHAPTER SEVENTEEN

1. MS. Nathan 466: Nathan to Brennan, 2 June 1916.
2. George Bernard Shaw, *The Matter With Ireland,* (ed. David Greene and Brian Laurence) London, 1962, pp. 112–13.
3. MS. Nathan 466: Nathan to Russell (A.E.), 30 May 1916.
4. MS. Nathan 477: Hannay to Nathan, 13 May 1916.
5. MS. Nathan 141: Dorothy Stopford to Nathan, 30 April 1916.
6. Dorothy Stopford's Papers: Nathan to Dorothy Stopford, 25 September 1916.
7. MS. Nathan 466: Nathan to Mrs S. Green, 13 May 1916.
8. MS. Nathan 477: Mrs S. Green to Nathan.
9. MS. Nathan 466: Nathan to Mrs S. Green, 4 June 1916.
10. MS. Nathan 477: Mrs S. Green to Nathan, 8 June 1916.
11. MS. Nathan 452–453: Mrs S. Green to Nathan, 25 January 1917.

CHAPTER NINETEEN

1. Dorothy Stopford's Papers: Nathan to Dorothy Stopford, 23 November 1917.
2. Ibid., 21 February 1917.
3. Nathan, op. cit., x.
4. Ervine, op. cit., p. 572.

SOURCES

I *Manuscript Material*

Nathan Papers (Bodleian Library).
Asquith Papers (Bodleian Library).
Byron, Leslie. *Opportunist Sinn Féiners*, London, 1921.
MS. Eng. Lett. E. 100 (Bodleian Library).
Haldane Papers (National Library of Scotland).
MacNeill Papers (National Library of Ireland, and Mrs Evelyn Tierney).
A. H. Norway's 'Irish Experiences in War' (Mrs F. M. Norway).
Mrs Alice Stopford Green's Papers (National Library of Ireland).
Dorothy Stopford's Papers (National Library of Ireland).

II *Printed Material*

NATHAN, SIR MATTHEW. Preface to *Annals of West Coker*. Cambridge,
    1937.
St Martin's Letter Bag. Post Office Headquarters, London, 1911.
Documents Relative to the Sinn Féin Movement (CMD. 1108 of 1921).
    H.M. Stationery Office, London.
On the Rebellion in Ireland (CMD. 8311 of 1916). Report of Royal
    Commission. H.M. Stationery Office, London.
'The Last Days of Dublin Castle', Blackwood's Magazine (London and
    Edinburgh), ccxii, No. 1732 (August, 1922), 137–190.
Sinn Féin Rebellion Handbook, Easter, 1916. Compiled by the Weekly
    Irish Times. Dublin, 1917.
NORWAY, MRS HAMILTON. *The Sinn Féin Rebellion As I Saw It*. Dublin,
    1916.
HEADLAM, MAURICE. *Irish Reminiscences*. London, 1947.
SHUTE, NEVIL. *Slide Rule*. London, 1954.

III *Newspapers and Periodicals*

*The Leader; Sinn Féin; New Ireland; Workers' Republic; Irish Freedom;
    Scissors and Paste; An Claidheamh Soluis; The Irish Volunteer;
    Ireland; The Spark; An tOglách, 1962; The Irish Times; Freeman's*

Journal; Irish Independent; Sunday Independent; Irish News; The Times (London).

IV *Other Printed Sources*

ARTHUR, SIR GEORGE. *General Sir John Maxwell.* London, 1932.
BAYLY, ADMIRAL SIR LEWIS. *Pull Together!* London, 1939.
BIRRELL, AUGUSTINE. *Things Past Redress.* London, 1937.
BONHAM CARTER, VIOLET. *Winston Churchill As I Knew Him.* London, 1965.
BULLOCH, JOHN. *M.I.5: Origin and History of the British Counter-Espionage Service.* London, 1963.
BYWATER, H. C. and FERRABY, H. C. *Strange Intelligence.* London, 1931.
CAMPBELL, OLWEN WARD. *Mary Kingsley.* London, 1957.
CAULFIELD, MAX. *The Easter Rebellion.* London, 1964.
CHAVASSE, MOIRIN. *Terence MacSwiney.* Dublin, 1961.
DEVOY, JOHN. *Recollections of an Irish Rebel.* New York, 1929.
ERVINE, ST JOHN. *Bernard Shaw.* London, 1956.
FERGUSSON, SIR JAMES. *The Curragh Incident.* London, 1964.
FIGGIS, DARRELL. *Recollections of the Irish War.* London, 1927.
FINGAL, COUNTESS OF. *Seventy Years Young.* Dublin, 1943.
FOX, R. M. *History of the Irish Citizen Army.* Dublin, 1943.
FRENCH, GERALD. *Life of Field-Marshal Sir John French.* London, 1931.
GOODSPEED, D. J. *The Conspirators, a Study of the Coup d'Etat.* London, 1962.
GREENE, DAVID and BRIAN LAURENCE. *The Matter with Ireland.* London, 1962.
GWYNN, DENIS. *The Life of John Redmond.* London, 1932.
——. *The Life and Death of Roger Casement.* London, 1931.
——. *History of Partition.* Dublin, 1950.
GWYNN, STEPHEN. *John Redmond's Last Years.* London, 1919.
HEALY, T. M. *Letters and Leaders of My Day.* London, 1928.
HOLT, EDGAR. *Protest in Arms.* London, 1960.
HOY, H. C. *40 O.B. or How the War Was Won.* London, 1932.
HYDE, H. MONTGOMERY. *Roger Casement (Famous Trials).* London, 1960.
JAMES, SIR WILLIAM M. *The Eyes of the Navy.* London, 1955.
JENKINS, ROY. *Asquith.* London, 1964.
LARKIN, EMMET. *James Larkin.* London, 1965.
LYNCH, D. and O'DONOGHUE, F. *The I.R.B. and the 1916 Insurrection.* Cork, 1957.
MACCOLL, RENE. *Roger Casement.* London, 1956.
MACARDLE, DOROTHY. *The Irish Republic.* Dublin, 1937.
MCDOWELL, R. B. *The Irish Administration, 1801–1914.* London, 1964.
MALONEY, WM. J. *The Forged Casement Diaries.* Dublin, 1936.
MARTIN, O.S.A., F. X. *The Howth Gun-Running.* Dublin, 1964.
——. *The Irish Volunteers, 1913–1915.* Dublin, 1963.

——. 'MacNeill on the 1916 Rising', Irish Historical Studies (Dublin), XII, No. 47 (March, 1961), 228–9, 241, 252.

MIDLETON, EARL OF. Ireland—Dupe or Heroine? London, 1932.

MONTEITH, ROBERT. Casement's Last Adventure. Dublin, 1953.

NIC SHIUBHLAIGH, MAIRE. The Splendid Years. Dublin, 1955.

O BRIAIN, LIAM. Cuimhní Cinn. Dublin, 1951.

O'BRIEN, CONOR CRUISE (ed.). The Shaping of Modern Ireland. London, 1960.

O'BRIEN, R. BARRY. Dublin Castle and the Irish People. London, 1909.

O'BRIEN, WILLIAM. Preface to JAMES CONNOLLY. Labour and Easter Week. Dublin, 1949.

——, and RYAN, DESMOND. Devoy's Post Bag. Vol. II. Dublin, 1963.

O'BROIN, LEON. Comhcheilg sa Chaisleán. Dublin, 1963.

O'DONOGHUE, F. Tomás MacCurtain. Tralee, 1958.

O'HEGARTY, P. S. History of Ireland Under the Union, 1801–1922. London, 1952.

PARMITER, GEOFFREY DE G. Roger Casement. London, 1936.

ROBINSON, SIR HENRY. Memories, Wise and Otherwise. London, 1923.

RYAN, A. P. Mutiny at the Curragh. London, 1956.

RYAN, DESMOND. The Rising. Dublin, 1949.

——. 1916 Poets. Dublin, 1963.

SINGLETON-GATES, PETER. The Black Diaries. London, 1959.

SPENDER, J. A., and ASQUITH, CYRIL. Life of Lord Oxford and Asquith. London, 1932.

SPINDLER, KARL. The Mystery of the Casement Ship. Re-issued with a foreword by Florence O'Donoghue. Tralee, 1956.

STEPHENS, JAMES. The Insurrection in Dublin. Dublin, 1916.

STREET, C. J. C. The Administration of Ireland. London, 1920.

THOMSON, SIR BASIL. Queer People. London, 1922.

WHITE, CAPTAIN J. R. Misfit. London, 1930.

WRENCH, JOHN EVELYN. Struggle 1914–1920. London, 1935.

INDEX

Aberdeen, Lady 22, 47
Aberdeen, Lord 22, 47
Ashe, Thomas 25
Asquith, H. H. 31, 45, 62, 70, 77, 100, 109–26, 130–6
Asquith, Violet 12, 49

Bailey, Daniel 83–4
Bailey, W. F. 39, 49, 57–8
Balfour, A. J. 16
Barnes, G. N. 177
Bayly, Sir Lewis 135, 137, 139–40
Beasly, Pierce 25
Bernstorff, Count von 142
Birrell, Augustine 15–18, 22, 24, 26, 27–8, 30–1, 38–40, 42–3, 46, 50–4, 56–8, 60, 62–6, 70–2, 74, 76, 78, 81–2, 84–5, 92, 98, 106, 111–18, 120, 136–7, 156–9, 161–2, 165, 167, 172–3
Blackwood, Lord Basil 106, 121
Blanco White, Amber 12, 175
Blayney, William 25
Blythe, Ernest 25, 69–71
Bonham Carter, Maurice 123, 131
Bourke, P. J. 59
Brade, R. H. 136
Brennan, Joseph 60–1, 160, 165

Campbell, James 77, 112, 131–2
Carson, Sir Edward 50, 132, 165, 176
Casement, Sir Roger 9–10, 20–1, 26, 28, 29, 31, 81–7, 89, 101, 114, 126, 133, 136–8, 141–2, 148, 155–6

Chalmers, Sir Robert 120, 123, 131, 163
Chamberlain, Joseph 12
Chamberlain, Sir Neville 28, 79, 137
Christensen, Adler 28
Churchill, Winston 30, 135
Clarke, Thomas J. 23, 33, 71, 74, 123, 142, 143, 154, 160, 168
Cochrane, Burke 28
Coffey, Denis J. 59
Colbert, C. 25
Collins, Cornelius 25, 32–4, 76, 81, 83, 148
Connolly, James 20, 25, 53, 74, 101, 114, 125–6, 143–5, 148, 150–1, 168
Conyngham, Lady Frederick 107
Cosgrave, W. T. 25
Cotton, A. W. 69–71
Cowan, Colonel H. V. 86
Crowly, J. P. 164

Daly, John 29, 33, 142, 154
De Valera, Edward 153
Devlin, Joseph 27, 46, 75, 76, 125
Devoy, John 138, 139, 142
Dillon, John 16, 27, 38–42, 45–7, 50, 55–6, 59, 63–4, 66, 71, 76–7, 80, 82, 85, 98, 102, 115, 118–20, 123–7, 130–3, 159

Edgeworth-Johnstone, W. 79, 86
Ervine, St John 59

Figgis, Darrel 29, 31, 160
Findlay, M. de C. 28

189

Fingall, Lady 49, 85–6
Fitzgibbon, John 25, 145
Fletcher, George 12
French, Lord 62–3, 70, 72–3, 76, 92, 109, 118, 123, 133, 135–6
Friend, General L. B. 27, 31, 42, 62–4, 71–3, 79, 86, 112, 115, 118, 136–7, 139, 157, 158–9, 160
Fullerton, Rev. Robert 29

George, David Lloyd 12, 17, 131, 176
Gill, T. P. 47, 170
Ginnell, L. 165
Gomersall, E. 95–6
Green, Alice Stopford 29–30, 75, 85, 170–2, 178
Gregory, Lady A. 13
Griffith, Arthur 25, 27

Haldane, Viscount 30, 51
Hall, Sir Reginald 31, 87, 138, 139, 142, 155, 160
Hannay, Canon J. O. 49, 153, 169
Hardinge of Penshurst, Lord 153, 160
Harrell, W. V. 24, 159
Headlam, Maurice 16, 99–100, 162–3
Hegarty, John 36–7
Hegarty, P. S. 35–6
Heppell-Marr, Constance 12, 174–5
Hobhouse, Charles 28, 33–4, 120, 162
Hobson, Bulmer 21, 25, 102, 143, 145, 147, 148
Holweig, Von Bethmann 143
Hoy, H. C. 138, 155
Hyde, Douglas 59, 80

Jackson, Sir H. B. 140
Jacobs, Miriam 11

Kelly, John T. 25
Kelly, Alderman Thomas 25, 79, 147, 168

Kent (Ceannt), Eamonn 25, 143, 145, 154
Kingsley, Mary 12, 178
Kitchener, Lord 26, 27, 50, 52, 110, 126
Kurten, G. P. 16, 60

Larkin, James 20, 25
Lewis, Major Owen 86
Little, P. J. 79
Long, Walter 43–5, 50, 132
Loreburn, Lord 65
Lowe, Superintendent 29
Lynch, Diarmuid 126, 143
Lyttleton, Lady 13

McBride, Major John 25
McCabe, Alex 65
McCullagh, Denis 29, 143
McDermott, John 125–6, 143, 148, 154
MacDonagh, Major General G. M. W. 135, 138, 139
MacDonagh, Thomas 59, 74, 80, 123, 144–8
McGooey, John 156
McMahon, James 14, 60
MacNeill, Eoin 25, 29–30, 59, 70, 83, 102, 109, 125, 137, 142–56
Magill, A. P. 82, 141, 164
Mahaffy, J. P. 172
Mahon, Lt.-Gen. Sir Bryan 31
Markievicz, Constance 25, 53, 97, 101, 110, 123, 167
Marmion, Abbot 125
Maxwell, Sir John 103, 110, 113, 115, 118–19, 123–7, 131–4
Mellowes, William 69–71
Meyer, Kuno 28
Midleton, Earl of 43, 54–5, 64–7, 109
Montagu, E. S. 118
Monteith, Robert 34, 74, 83, 148, 156
Moore, Colonel Maurice 43
Moran, D. P. 14
Murray, Sir Evelyn 29

Nathan, Estelle 78, 85, 87, 104–8
Nathan, Jonah 11
Nathan, Sir Matthew, Family background, 11; Colonial and Home appointments, 12; designated Under-Secretary for Ireland, 12; Irish reactions, 14–16; Birrell's Irish policy, 17; the political and industrial situation, 19–31; disloyalty in the Civil Service, 32–7; the seditious press, 38–45; the Coalition Government, 50–1; Sinn Féiners make progress, 52–3; O'Donovan Rossa funeral, 53; G. B. Shaw's *O'Flaherty V.C.*, 56–9; Unionist pressure, 64–7; Wimborne asserts himself, 68; deportations, 69–71; does not believe Sinn Féin leaders intend insurrection, 72–8; letter tells of rising projected for Easter Eve, 1916, 79; an alleged Castle document, 79–80; the Casement episode, 80–5; conferences in the Viceregal, 84–8; trapped in Dublin Castle, 9–10 and 90–1; the Rising, 91–117; resigns with Birrell, 117–19; Royal Commission of Enquiry, 141–61; letters following resignation, 162–73; Constance Heppell-Marr and Amber Blanco White, 174–5; reports for duty to Military Authority, 176; subsequent career, 176–8
Nathan, Maude 104–8
Nathan, Pamela 104–8
Needham, Raymond 76, 164
Norway, Arthur Hamilton 9–10, 14–15, 32–6, 47, 87–103, 119, 122
Norway, Fred 89, 122
Norway, Mrs Mary Louisa 89, 95, 96

Norway, Nevil (Shute) 89, 95

O'Brien, Ignatius 121
O'Connell, J. J. 145, 147, 148
O'Connor, Sir James 93–4, 112, 163
O'Dea, Bishop 47
O'Donovan Rossa 53
O'Flanagan, Father Michael 64
O'Keeffe, Patrick 32–3
O'Rahilly, The 153

Parmoor, Lord 54, 65
Pearse, Margaret 128, 131
Pearse, Mrs 127–31
Pearse, P. H. 21, 25, 53, 101, 113, 123, 127–31, 143–9, 154, 168
Pearse, Willie 123, 129–31
Pease, Joseph Albert 120–2
Plunkett, Sir Horace 49, 85, 132, 163, 177
Plunkett, Joseph 143, 145, 147, 154, 155
Price, Major Ivor H. 9–10, 29, 73–4, 81, 86, 87, 90–3, 125, 127, 136–7, 148, 153, 159, 160, 163

Redmond, John 24, 25, 27, 31, 38, 41, 43, 45, 47, 50–6, 64, 68, 75, 76, 80, 85, 102, 109, 115, 118–19, 124, 125, 133, 159, 162
Robertson, Sir W. 109
Russell, George (AE) 13, 49, 167, 170
Russell, T. W. 92, 165

Samuel, Herbert 15
Scott, Lady Kathleen 49
Selbourne, Lord 43, 132
Shaw, George Bernard 56–8, 165–7, 178
Sheehy Skeffington, Francis 25, 66, 102, 131
Simon, Sir John 30
Somers, Elizabeth N. 34
Stack, Austin 34–5, 81, 83, 148

Stafford, Brigadier W. F. H. 79, 111,
    136–7, 139, 157, 160
Starkie, W. J. M. 47, 162
Stopford, Dorothy 85, 104, 137,
    169–70, 176, 177, 178
Sweetman, Father 125
Synge, John Millington 12

Thompson, Basil 92
Wimborne, Lord 31, 51–2, 55, 68–9,
    74, 82–8, 97, 101, 110, 111,
    116, 118, 119–23, 132, 136,
    137, 161

Yeats, W. B. 13, 31